DEDICATION

I dedicate this book to Dr. Yan Xin.
Without him, it wouldn't have happened.

Denim Brick Publications

312 Water Street

Vancouver, BC

Canada

V6B 1B6

ISBN 979-8-5765-7428-5

CONTENTS

INTRODUCTION

This book isn't a bit of fun or a way to pass some time. If that's what you're after, quit reading now and go watch your favourite soap opera, videos on YouTube, or a reality show. There's plenty of such entertainment in the world already — maybe too much! This book is for people who are serious about life. It's for people seeking answers to questions like:

- What is a good human life?

- How can my life become better?

- How can we make society better for everyone?

- What's the value, purpose, or meaning of life?

Socrates said that happiness is humanity's ultimate desire.[1] Aristotle said happiness is the goal of life, the highest good.[2] Two thousand years later, American philosopher William James echoed them, saying "how to gain, how to keep, how to recover happiness, is in fact for most men at all times the secret motives of all they do, and of all they are willing to endure."[3] Although there are arguments about whether happiness is life's most valuable thing[4], it's safe to say that as humans, happiness is very important to us. It has been the subject of countless treatises, dialogues, and books for over two millennia.

Yet, surprisingly, there are still no definite answers to seemingly simple questions like "What is happiness?" and "How can we achieve it?"

As in medical science, a correct diagnosis is half a cure. I believe that understanding happiness is fundamental in answering further questions. After all, if we can't define happiness, how can we begin to value it or look to attain it? Trying to answer these questions without first defining happiness seems absurd and futile to me. This book, then, looks to answer one core question: **What is happiness?**

What this book contains

Isaac Newton said, "if I have seen further than others, it is by standing upon the shoulders of giants". It's not this author's intention to liken himself to a great scientist such as Newton through merely quoting him, but it is true to say that this book has relied on and benefited from the countless works and ideas of giants past and present. These giants include not only great minds who directly contributed to the millennia-long discourse on happiness, but also those sages from different cultures whose influence on my thinking is equally deep.

I am also grateful to the modern-day researchers and scholars who meticulously map the terrains we traverse in search of answers about human happiness. There are many who are not directly referenced in this book but whose help in nurturing my thinking has played a crucial part in its foundation. That said, this book does not lack creative ideas of its own. The last thing I want to do is plagiarise.

For clarity's sake, I offer a brief outline of the book here. Its purpose is to recognise which ideas are my own and which belong to others. Where I cannot be sure of either originality or influence, I have deferred to influence. If you want to read this book without knowing the journey ahead of you, feel free to move on to chapter 1.

Chapter 1 is a brief review and classification of definitions of happiness prior to this book. I cannot give enough credit to Professor D. McMahon, whose magnificent book *Happiness: A History*[5], was a big influence. The majority of this chapter is filtered from his extensive review of classical definitions of happiness, from Ancient Greece to the mid-20th century. The only aspect I claim as original is the classification and grouping of definitions into two main camps: philosophical hedonistic and idealistic.

Chapter 2 is a dissection of the life we live and how happiness is experienced in this life. In recent years, researchers have clearly distinguished between the happiness that people feel from moment to moment and when evaluating a part of life (job satisfaction, marital satisfaction, etc.) or when reflecting on or assessing life as a whole.[6]

It's further clarified in this chapter that happiness is an *experience*, not a moral or value concept such as justice or virtue. The new contribution made by this book is the offer of an answer to how we experience happiness in life. We experience happiness with our awareness or our faculties of awareness. The first major original idea I present is that there are four or five levels of human awareness in our daily life experiences: our bodily awareness, emotional awareness, thought awareness, ethical awareness, and perhaps spiritual awareness. Construing life experience through a process similar to a tribunal, with four or five levels (members) of human awareness, is inspired by and borrowed from an Eastern understanding of human life.[7]

Chapter 3 is the core of this book's theory; the foundation on which the remaining text is built on and evolves from. The definition of happiness is the origin of all other original ideas in this book. It is a general theory of happiness believed to underline all previous definitions of happiness, from Ancient Greece to the present-day subjective well-being.[8;9;10;11]

The closest definition of happiness to the one presented here is probably Epicurus' understanding of happiness, particularly his negative pleasure of the state of **aponia** (absence of bodily pain) and the state of **ataraxia** (absence of mental anguish or anxiety).[12] However, Epicurus understood human happiness not as a dynamic equilibrium, but as an isolated event in both his positive and negative pleasures — or his definitions of them. He regarded only experiences to alleviate bodily pains, such as hunger, as a positive pleasure. What we might define as positive pleasures today, such as entertainment, he regarded as activities in vain.

His negative pleasures were so rare that he declared that people who acquired them in the long term "rivalled Zeus" in their happiness. [12] Thus, in Epicurus' terms, very few things in human life are pleasures and meaningful. Even Flow (a term first coined by Csikszentmihalyi[13] to describe the mental condition and experience when a person performing an activity is fully immersed in feelings of total focus, full involvement, and enjoyment in the process, more details in Chapter 6,) which is claimed as an optimal life experience[13], or positive engagement with people would be regarded as activities in vain. This might explain why Epicurus advocated reclusion from human society as the means to reaching happiness.[12] The happiness defined in this book has to be understood from a dynamic equilibrium of positive and negative sides. The negative side is fetters.

This chapter explains the fundamental difference between this book's understanding of pleasure–happiness and all previous theories found in both hedonic and idealistic definitions of happiness. All previous pleasure–happiness theories view positive and negative experiences separately, focusing only on the positive side to seek an understanding and explanation of pleasure–happiness. This book proposes a theory to view and understand pleasure–happiness from a dynamic equilibrium of both positive and negative sides.

In a paradigm shift in the human understanding of life, pleasure–happiness is understood as a short episode in a never-ending tug-of-war between the positive and negative in human awareness and experience. The stories and cases cited are common human experiences, but they reveal fresh meanings when viewed from a new angle.

The happiness theory hypothesized in this book explains that the fundamental differences between hedonic definitions of happiness (i.e. pleasure) and idealistic definitions of happiness are only relative to freedom from fetters. One (pleasure) is partial freedom or incomplete freedom from fetters, whilst the other (ideal) is complete freedom from fetters. (Fetters is a key concept specifically defined and expanded on to understand the happiness hypothesis proposed in this book. There is more detailed and extensive discussion on the concept of fetters in Chapters 3, 4, and 5.)

Chapter 4 closely examines human fetters. Fetters are dominant and pervasive in human life, playing a more important role in determining levels of happiness than the other side of the dynamic equilibrium: positive engagement with people or activities. When occupied by positive engagement with people or activities, we forget about our troubles — our fetters — and are temporarily free of them. Thus, both Epicurus' positive and negative pleasures are included in our definition of happiness as being free from fetters. Removing a fetter, such as hunger or thirst, in Epicurus' positive pleasures will be a classic case of freedom as defined here. The states of aponia or ataraxia are long-lasting freedom from fetters achievable only by the rare likes of sages, and are much longer than Flow (long-lasting pleasure for ordinary people).[13]

Beyond Epicurus' positive and negative pleasures, all common pleasurable activities such as entertainment, healthy hobbies, or reading an interesting book can be easily understood as happiness experienced in real life from our definition of human happiness.

"Fetter" is a common English word I've adopted and expanded specifically to cover all negative feelings, things, or events that cause negative experiences in human life. Most fetters are almost "common sense", obvious to most people without requiring much explanation. The contribution of this book is to clarify and group them into categories for the convenience of understanding and discussing human life and happiness. In this first chapter on the subject, I examine external fetters, that is, the things that are external to us that affect our happiness.

It must be recognised that Epicurus' states of aponia and ataraxia allude to similar ideas of "bodily pains and mental anguish or anxiety" as does our definition of fetters. It could be claimed that Epicurus' notions are further developed, expanded, and clarified in the concept of fetters in this book. This can be viewed from two main perspectives. The first is that the human fetters defined here cover more than just "bodily pains and mental anguish or anxiety". For example, life-maintaining desires such as hunger and thirst aside, desires are generally regarded as unnatural needs and so are not treated as bodily pains in Epicurus' terms. Here, however, desires are treated as human fetters if they cause pain or uneasiness when unsatisfied.

The major contribution of this book regarding human fetters is further clarifying, categorising, and developing Epicurus' "bodily pains and mental anguish or anxiety" after two millennia of siesta. Armed with this, we will be able to identify and understand the obstacles that prevent us from living a happy life.

Chapter 5 looks at the more pervasive and significant fetters that affect our happiness — the internal fetters of mental anguish, illness, and desires. Several ideas require crediting here. The first is Mihaly Csikszentmihalyi's idea of chaotic thought as part of mental fetters. In fact, Csikszentmihalyi gave a detailed and clear description of this fetter in his original book on Flow.[13]

It's worth noting that chaotic thinking, which I argue forms the main mental fetter for humans, is not considered in Epicurus' mental anguish or anxiety until it reaches a level of mental abnormality.

Desire as a fetter is not an original idea of this book; it was declared so in classic Stoic philosophies[14,15] over 2000 years ago and elucidated by Schopenhauer in his masterpiece *The World as Will and Representation*.[16] However, it is first proposed here that a desire becomes a fetter only when it causes pain if not satisfied.

Chapter 6 further discusses and clarifies positive experiences in human life and the most important processes that humans derive pleasure–happiness from. It has been understood since Aristotle[2;8], and perhaps even earlier, that positive engagement with people is important to human happiness. However, the underlying mechanism governing why has never been fully understood. This book explains why positive relationships, whether in family or social environments, are so important to human pleasure–happiness.

The idea of Flow was conceptualized by Csikszentmihalyi,[13] and the ideas for all of the book's discussions about Flow have been borrowed from him, re-narrated, and used to illustrate the theory hypothesized here with personal experiences. The only contribution from the author regarding Flow is the emphasis on a deep interest in or engagement with a given activity. Only deep absorption in an activity provides the person in Flow with relief–forgetfulness from the fetters in their life.

Sub-Flow is an original idea first proposed here. Csikszentmihalyi's Flow concept depicts optimal life experiences accurately.[13] However, Flow processes only account for a tiny fraction of experiences in human life, at least in time spent on them in our daily lives. Contrary to Csikszentmihalyi, who tried to categorise them as Flow processes[13], most important life processes, such as school learning and work are mainly sub-Flow processes.

In Flow, the process itself is the focus, whereas in sub-Flow, the goal is the focus. The vast majority of human activities belong to sub-Flow processes. Seeking success is a near-universal goal and the processes by which we seek success are mainly sub-Flow ones. What we need or want are our desires or aspirations, the satisfaction of which forms the purpose of all we do in our lives. If the processes to satisfy or fulfil desires or aspirations are pleasing to us, they are pleasures or even Flow. The rest are sub-Flow processes.

Chapter 7 is about the large-scale misunderstanding of what happiness is. The delusion of money suggested in this chapter is not original; "money can't buy you happiness" is even something of a cliché. However, only through understanding life as the process of a dynamic equilibrium do the real reasons why money can never buy us (long-lasting) happiness become clear.

Grand-scale corruption as an example of the delusion of money is an original idea in this book. Conventionally, grand-scale corruption is understood as a big threat to the health and stability of a society, but we almost take it for granted that the perpetrators of such crimes get the benefits of vast sums of money at the expense of the state or general public. It is this book's contention that such perpetrators get no real benefit where their own happiness is concerned. If it seems that they do, it's a delusion.

The delusion of success is another original idea of this book that may shake the foundations of the conventional convictions that the vast majority of people build their world views and values on. The author may well antagonize the whole of society, not just intellectual circles, with this idea because it contradicts the basic, lifelong beliefs of ordinary people. However, it's not the intention to create sensational headlines. Rather, it's hoped as a wake-up call to the collective slumber of a society seeking happiness in the wrong place.

Mid-life crises have been debated and studied for over half a century. Gail Sheehy featured an outstanding study about them in her book *Passages*[17] and included a comprehensive description of this phenomenon. I have to attribute most of my understanding of mid-life crises in this chapter to her. However, I have explained mid-life crises within the paradigm of the theory of happiness proposed here.

The unique contribution made by this book, which is pivotal in understanding the mid-life crisis, is "loss of goals when successes are reached" — the main issue of a mid-life crisis. In many places in Sheehy's book[17], she was almost there but failed to dig out the root. "Loss of goals" is the key to a mid-life crisis. This discovery is only possible after understanding most life processes as sub-Flow ones in which goals are key.

Chapter 8 provides a discussion on the various theories that have attempted to quantify or calculate happiness such as Bentham's utilities, GDP, and others. The unique proposition here is a new calculation of pleasure–happiness so that it belongs to political economy, or economy, more than philosophy. Again, the methodology suggested in this book is a paradigm shift from conventional methods in quantifying well-being or happiness.[18]

Chapter 9 provides examples where the theory proposed in this book can be applied to explain issues evident in the latest research on happiness. It's intended for academic readers, specifically those who are attempting to tackle outstanding issues, particularly in the field of subjective well-being. As with any scientific or philosophical theory, the ultimate criteria of its validity is a "reality check". Using the theory advocated in this book, this chapter provides that reality check for the cutting-edge academic research of happiness.

Chapter 10 is a fun and happy ending to the book. We are all curious about who the happiest people on this planet are and why. Though some philosophers, such as Schopenhauer, had ideas about what truly happy people look like mentally[16], no one can be certain who is or was the happiest person that ever lived. Ultimately, the "have nots" have counted more than the "haves" in the happiness arena of human life.

Chapter 1:

Happiness Definitions Reviewed and Classified

Happiness is one of the most important issues in human life and likely the most-discussed subject in the history of philosophy. In fact, Western philosophy probably originated from dialogues about happiness in Greece some 2,500 years ago.[5] Since then, countless philosophers have contemplated the subject. Books and treatises have been written in all kinds of languages, filling libraries in every corner of the globe. As Darrin McMahon wrote in his outstanding book *Happiness: A History,*[5] to compile every theory of happiness ever hypothesized in literature would be impossible. Fortunately, this book focuses solely on the concept of what happiness *is*, reducing our discussion to the key points of related theories. I have omitted any discussion of theories around other ideas such as how to *be* happy.

My selection of classical theories of happiness in Western philosophy relies almost entirely on McMahon's book. As for more recent theories, I will focus on some of the most-discussed and widely accepted theories in mainstream philosophy, psychology, and economics. It must be remembered that the definitions reviewed here are subjective rather than exhaustive. I have chosen them as they best represent mainstream ideas in the exploration of happiness.

Mark Martin classified happiness definitions as Desire Satisfaction, Hedonistic, Life Satisfaction, and Normative.[19] I prefer to divide all happiness theories into two larger camps. The first can be called **philosophical hedonistic** definitions. The main characteristic of such definitions is their acceptance or recognition of pleasures known to ordinary people in daily life as happiness or kinds of happiness. The second can be called **idealistic**. The most distinctive characteristic of idealistic definitions of happiness is their refusal to accept pleasures as happiness. Instead, such definitions propose "real" happiness to be found in a state or condition. Another reason why these theories of happiness are called idealistic is because the conditions or states described are so idealised and difficult to achieve that — if they exist at all — they're incredibly rare. Idealistic definitions of happiness differ only in the *specifics* of the state or condition constituting their proposed ideal.

The Ancient Greek definitions

Socrates believed that all human beings desire happiness. His definition of happiness is the "intercourse between the lover of wisdom and truth, a sort of intellectual organism in which desire is sated and happiness flows forth… That, if ever, is the moment when life is worth living."[20] Socrates rejected all previous Greek conceptions of what it meant to be happy, declaring that "happiness is not hedonism, and nor is it ultimately to be found in good fortune, pleasure, power, riches, fame, even health, or family love."[20] Socrates's definition of happiness is typically idealistic. In today's world, if seeking knowledge and truth with the right order of the soul and completely disciplined Eros is the only happiness, then even most philosophers don't qualify for it — let alone those living lives remote from the ideal state that Socrates described.

Plato's definition of happiness is also idealistic, but in different ways from his beloved teacher and mentor. Plato spoke of collective happiness as an ideal world where the philosopher is the king, their soul in constant harmony with the divine. The rest of the Republic will be in their right places, in harmony with themselves and each other. Plato rejected pleasures as happiness because most men don't know what is best for them, leaving them prone to the lowest appetites, and often leading to chaos.[20] Plato's view of happiness as a collective, idealistic world was shared by Ancient Eastern philosophers such as Confucius and Lao Zhu, who also downplayed any personal sense of happiness we might recognise today, instead advocating an ideal world of ordered and harmonious societies lead by wise sages.

The concept of an idealistic world and society has been revisited throughout history, be it through utopianism, the French Revolution, or communism. The failure of all kinds of utopian communes and the catastrophic consequences of communist practices in countries with a variety of cultural backgrounds reminds us that Plato's happy world remains idealistic.

Aristotle's definition of happiness is also idealistic, but with a little more acceptance of ordinary ideas around what a happy life consists of. Firstly, he concluded that happiness is the highest good and the ultimate end ("telos") of human life.[2] Secondly, he believed that happiness is a result of a human life well-lived. By well-lived, he meant a life of virtues from birth to death.

Like his mentors Socrates and Plato, Aristotle felt that virtues were the most important element of a happy life. However, he rejected the idea that virtue alone could constitute happiness in any given situation, saying "someone might possess virtue, but still suffer the worst evils and misfortunes." He also rejected the notion of pleasures as happiness but admitted that "good fortunes such as a good birth, money, friends, children, and physical beauty are necessary conditions to happiness."[2]

He believed that a virtuous life would achieve at best only the second class of happiness.[2] The first, and highest, class of happiness is pure contemplation, the only action shared by both gods and men. Both of Aristotle's classes of happiness as a life well-lived (a life of virtue from birth until death) and of pure contemplation are idealistic compared to contemporary theories of happiness such as subjective well-being.[11] Very few people living today would qualify for either of Aristotle's definitions of happiness. Therefore, Aristotle's happiness may be great, but it remains an ideal for us to only strive for.

Epicurus was probably the first well-known philosopher in Western philosophical history to recognise pleasures as happiness, so his happiness theory is classified, at least partially, as philosophical hedonism. It's worth pointing out here that philosophical hedonism is not the same as hedonism in the colloquial sense, which was formally known as "folk hedonism". Folk hedonism is a lifestyle that regards pleasure, particularly bodily pleasure through the sense organs, as the central and ultimate goal of life. It has an implied approval of self-centred actions as long as they bring pleasures to the individual, regardless of morality. Lavish, excessive lifestyles are logical and normal in this kind of hedonism but would be questionable in even the most relaxed of philosophical hedonisms, such as utilitarianism and subjective well-being.[11]

Only a minority of philosophers endorse the view that seeking self-centred pleasures is the one concern of happiness, regardless of anything else. Philosophical hedonism regards pleasures as happiness, or at least some form of it, but it is specific about which kinds of pleasures

(Epicureanism) or whose (utilitarianism's belief in the happiness of the largest number of people over of that of the individual).

Pleasure, in Epicurus' words, is not "of profligates or that which lies in sensuality [but] freedom from bodily pain and mental anguish."[12] In other words, pleasure defined negatively as the absence of bodily pain, mental anguish, or anxiety. From Epicurus' perspective, the vast majority of human desires are idle, empty, or irrelevant, with very few (the desires to relieve hunger, quench thirst, and keep warm) being necessary or natural for pleasure.

It may surprise us today to learn that socialising over a three-course dinner at a high-end restaurant is not a pleasure in Epicurus' terms. For him, pleasure would be an everyday, homemade, plain meal to feed a hungry man. Likewise, almost all of the activities we regard today as pleasures, such as watching our favourite TV shows, playing games, or participating in speculative sports, would not be pleasures in Epicurean terms but actions or events in vain.

No matter how strange this definition of pleasure seems to us today, Epicurus' definition of pleasure as happiness (and because the things he defined as pleasures are obtainable by ordinary people) qualifies Epicureanism as philosophical hedonism.

That said, Epicurus defined two types of pleasure: positive pleasure, which gives us sensations, and negative pleasure, which is the absence of bodily pain (what he called aponia) and the absence of mental anguish or anxiety (what he called ataraxia). Epicurus believed that negative pleasure was superior to positive. However, negative pleasure, aponia, or ataraxia lasting for more than a few seconds is impossible for ordinary people (this will be discussed more later). Epicurus realised this, stating that people who achieved lasting aponia and/or ataraxia rival Zeus in their happiness. Negative pleasure, the higher pleasure, is an ideal state for human beings. From this point, the Epicurean approach of happiness can also be called idealistic. Therefore, in defining happiness, Epicureanism can be said to be part-philosophical-hedonism, part-idealistic.

With its total denial of the role of pleasures in happiness, Stoicism is believed to be the opposite of Epicureanism. It preaches that only virtue is required for happiness. In fact, it goes as far as claiming that virtue *is* happiness![21] Martin classified the Stoic definition of happiness as normative.[19] Normative theories exist largely in the realm of ethics, concerning questions of should vs. should not, right vs. wrong, etc. Most of the classical teachings of sages from different cultures are normative and consider whether there is a "right" way to live our lives. For example, the Bible is the norm and "right" way of life for both Jewish and Christian living (for example, the Ten Commandments), in the same way that the Quran sets the rules of living for Muslims, and so on. In the same realm of ethics, Kant's philosophy focuses largely on the subject of right vs. wrong, but from a secular (non-religious) standpoint.

Above all else, Stoicism is a theory concerned with how we *should* live our lives and prescribes virtue as its only remedy, tool, and road. In today's mainstream understanding of happiness and subjective well-being, virtue (often related to ultraism) is the opposite of happiness — where happiness is defined as enjoying a moment of pleasure. Thus, the Stoic's definition of happiness is idealistic in achieving happiness — with virtue being achievable by none but saints and sages.

The philosophy of Stoicism continued into the Roman Empire with proponent Marcus Aurelius, then declined in popularity due to the ascendance of Christianity.

Religious definitions

The classical Christian definition of happiness could be regarded as idealistic. Happiness is so ideal in classical Christian terms that it is not possible on earth and exists only in heaven after this life is over. In St Augustine's words, "Happiness is fullness or plenitude flowing in such a way that the one who experiences it lacks nothing, knows no want. Those who are happy are not in need but are filled with the supreme measure of wisdom. To be happy is thus to be suffused with truth, to have God within the soul, to enjoy God." [22]

Thomas Aquinas agreed with St Augustine that perfect happiness ("beatitude") comes only with death and heaven, but that there is imperfect happiness ("felicitas") on earth: the contemplation of truth. Like Aristotle before him, Aquinas believed that "man's ultimate happiness consists in the contemplation of truth, for this operation is specific to man and is shared with no animals. Also, it is not directed to any other end since the contemplation of truth is sought for its own sake.

In this operation man is united to higher beings (substances) since this is the only human operation that is carried out both by God and the separate substances (angels)." However, Aquinas was quick to emphasise that "the purest form of this reflection will come only in heaven."[23]

Christian reformists did not deviate very much from their Catholic predecessors in defining happiness, with true happiness being accessible only in heaven. However, the way to this climax is through the grace of God, which is bestowed upon just men of faith. "Joy and good feeling, conversely, could be treated as an indication of divine favour. The experience of happiness on earth — unsullied merriment and Christian joy — was an outward sign of God's grace... To pursue happiness was to seek signs of assurance of future felicity."[5] One aspect of Protestant doctrine, Calvinistic predestination (that God has chosen a relatively small number of souls to be saved through grace), limits the hope of happiness to none but a few.[24]

Definitions of happiness concerning mystical practices in the Christian tradition are worth mentioning here. Instead of only the hope of beatitude in heaven, Pseudo-Dionysius, Boethius, and Erigena presented a mysterious ascending of the soul to face God, or a "union" with God through mystic bliss whilst on Earth.[25] Such practices aren't exclusive to the Christian tradition. Sufism in Islam has similar, if not identical, practices.[26] The concept of union with God is known similarly but less dogmatically as "nirvana" in Buddhism, "mahasamādhi" in Hinduism, and "spiritual death" in Taoism. All of these traditions seemingly point to a union with such a being as the highest achievement and ultimate happiness of an individual.

This concept reaches much wider than religion in Eastern traditions. In traditional Indian yoga practices, the very word "yoga" translates as "union". Yoga includes bhakti yoga (focused on the cultivation of love and devotion toward God), jñāna yoga (liberation through knowledge), karma yoga (achieving perfection in selfless action), and raja yoga (liberation through meditation).[27] Thus, yoga encompasses a much wider range of human life than religious practice. As such, union with God seems like a universal goal in mystical practices (or at least mainstream mystical practice, if such a thing exists). Of course, such ultimate happiness is purely idealistic by today's definitions of happiness.

Enlightenment age definitions

John Locke was a major thinker among Renaissance humanists, who defined the main characteristics of modern Western societies to this day. He believed that happiness formed one end of human existence, with misery forming the other.[28] For Locke, human life was a perpetual, pendulum-like movement. Happiness in its full extent is therefore the utmost pleasure we are capable of, and misery the utmost pain. Locke dismissed ancient, idealistic definitions of placing happiness solely in virtue or contemplation, but he offered no clear definition himself beyond happiness being the ultimate pleasure of a human. Locke placed his happiness bet on beatitude, so he's certainly an idealist when it comes to defining happiness.

Another Enlightenment giant, Jean-Jacques Rousseau was also idealistic in his definition of happiness. Rousseau vehemently denied pleasures as happiness, saying "even in our keenest pleasures there is scarcely a single moment of which the heart could truthfully say: 'Would that this moment could last forever!' How can we give the name of happiness to a fleeting state which leaves our hearts still empty and anxious, either regretting something past or desiring something that is yet to come?"[29] He admitted that when it came to happiness, "all seek it, and none finds it" and believed that "it involved neither great pleasures nor newly enlightened truths."

It was rather a state of perfect wholeness and plenitude of being in which Rousseau felt himself a "self-sufficient like God"[29] of the island of Saint-Pierre, where he lived when in exile, and "where the soul can find a resting place secure enough to establish itself and concentrate its entire being there, with no need to remember the past or reach into future, where time is nothing to it, where the present runs on indefinitely but this duration goes unnoticed, with no sign of the passing of time, and no other feeling of depreciation or enjoyment, pleasure or pain, desire or fear than simply the feeling of existence, a feeling that fills our soul entirely, as long as this state lasts, we can call ourselves happy, not with a poor, incomplete and relative happiness such as we find in the pleasures of life, but with a sufficiently complete and perfect happiness which leaves no emptiness to be filled in the soul."[29] Rousseau's happiness is idealistic to the point that he himself admitted that the happy state he described when he was on the island of Saint-Pierre might have been a figment of his imagination.

Thomas Hobbes, a contemporary of Locke, could be classified as a complete philosophical hedonist in his definition of happiness. In fact his happiness could even be termed hedonism in the conventional sense. Felicity (happiness) was "continual progress of the desire, from one object to another, the attaining of the former being still but the way to the latter... Continual success in obtaining those things which a man from time to time desireth, that is to say, continual prospering, is that men called Felicity; I mean the felicity of this life. For there is no such thing as perpetual tranquillity of mind, while we live here; because life itself is but motion, and can never be without desire, nor without fear, no more than without sense." [30] In Hobbes' view, human bodies could only be at rest when all motion stopped. Until that time, they would be ruled by a "perpetual and restless desire of power after power, that ceaseth only in death." [30]

Industrial era definitions

Bentham's utilitarianism is classical philosophical hedonism in its definition of happiness. Since its inception, utilitarianism has achieved tremendous success in a variety of ways. It may be surprising to learn that utilitarianism is largely a theory of ethics, originally intended to provide a foundation for human laws. It's still a cornerstone of today's civil laws and their everyday applications. Bentham himself may have been surprised to see two of the most influential intellectual groups in today's societies, namely economists and psychologists, wholeheartedly adopting his concepts of utility (in economic theories that regard an individual's goal as being to maximise their utilities in life) and pleasure–happiness (in the psychological study of subjective well-being). The central tenet of utilitarianism is "the largest happiness for the largest number of people." [31] Bentham regarded pleasures as happiness, from noble "high" pleasures such as Socrates' seeking of truth by contemplating, to "low" pleasures such as drinking cheap alcohol in a sleazy bar, with a gentle reminder that one person's enjoyment should not impede another's happiness. [31]

Schopenhauer was notorious for his unprecedentedly pessimistic view of human happiness. He mocked not only the Romantics but also Locke and Rousseau, reckoning their notion that "we exist in order to be happy" was the only "inborn error." [16] The "will to life" claimed by Schopenhauer as the vital force that animates all life was "not a seed of joy planted within, waiting to be given nourishment and bloom, but only a germinating source of pain. Imbedded in our very person is the kernel of all despair." [16]

True happiness, in Schopenhauer's terms, is "a type of secular beatitude or nirvana, that ocean-like calmness of the spirit, that deep tranquility, that unshakable confidence and serenity, whose mere reflection in the countenance…is a complete and certain gospel."[16] Thus, Schopenhauer's definition of happiness is also idealistic and barely possible in human lives.

Hegel pointed to an "unhappy consciousness" or "the alienated soul" as the source of human unhappiness. Such conditions condemned humans to live in conflict within themselves and with each other. Hegel's genuine happiness was man "in harmony with himself." "The Final Realization, the Full Flowering of Freedom. The Ultimate Realization would be social. Final Freedom, that is, would entail not just the overcoming of individual alienation — reconciling men and women to nature and themselves — but also the overcoming of social alienation, reconciling men and women to each other. In the context of a close-knit, organic community, the freedom of each would be bound up with the freedom of all."[5] Hegel's happiness, the ultimate freedom for one and all, is so remote from today's reality and from the collective achievements of all social strivings toward that end until today (capitalism, socialism, and communism) that it can only be viewed as purely idealistic.

Contemporary definitions

Contemporary mainstream theories of happiness are still mainly divided into two camps: philosophical hedonistic and idealistic. The former are mainly economic theories whose main focus is utility. A good example from this camp is Richard Layard, whose definition of happiness is clearly philosophical hedonistic, just like that of his idol and fellow countryman Jeremy Bentham.[11] In his book *Happiness: Lessons from a New* Science, Layard unapologetically defended pleasures as happiness and utilitarianism's largest happiness for the largest number approach.[11]

Psychologists, on the other hand, are more inclined to be idealistic in their overall tone. Mihaly Csikszentmihalyi's definition of Flow, the optimum life experience, is idealistic in a typically modern sense.[13] Flow is a mental condition in which a person performing an activity is fully immersed in a feeling of total focus, full involvement, and enjoyment in the process of a given activity. Whilst not as unattainable as Schopenhauer's "everlasting tranquillity", Flow is still a luxury enjoyed by few in society, and only then in specific activities.

Matthieu Ricard, the French biologist-turned-Tibetan Buddhist, is also idealistic in his understanding and definition of happiness. "Happiness can't be limited to a few pleasant sensations, to some intense pleasure, to an eruption of joy or a fleeting sense of serenity, to a cherry day or a magic moment that sneaks upon us in the labyrinth of our existence. Such diverse facets are not enough in themselves to build an accurate image of the profound and lasting fulfilment that characterizes true happiness... By happiness, [I] mean a deep sense of flourishing that arises from an exceptionally healthy mind. This is not a mere pleasurable feeling, a fleeting emotion, or a mood, but an optimal state of being. Happiness is also a way of interpreting the world."[32]

Today, the main approaches of philosophers and psychologists in defining happiness blend philosophical hedonistic and idealistic ideas. As the predominant culture in today's intellectual cycles is to avoid instruction (i.e. telling people what their happiness *should* be), most philosophers and psychologists accept pleasures as happiness in the same way that average people would. That said, they are also reluctant to accept or reduce happiness to pleasures or pleasures only, which Aristotle regarded as the "Telos" (ultimate good) of humans. Because of this, they often expand or elevate the concept of happiness to a more dignified level than mundane pleasures to make happiness more acceptable.

Martin Seligman, the founder of "positive psychology", is one such person. Seligman accepted pleasures and gratifications as authentic happiness,[33] yet he used a large part of his book on the subject to add many signature strengths (virtues) to modify and decorate the concept of authentic happiness. Indeed, Seligman became dissatisfied with his own theory of authentic happiness as a good life (well-being) and changed his definition to "flourish", which adds engagement, relationships, meaning, and accomplishment to happiness.[34]

Flourish has an aura of self-realisation with ethical meaning that was lacking in his original "authentic happiness". It's undeniable that a life of flourish is better than a life consisting solely of positive emotions. However, if flourish is the only life that can be regarded as a life of well-being, then the vast majority of the population do not have it, especially when considering how few have the luxury of even contemplating flourish amid their daily struggle to survive. This makes Seligman's definition of well-being idealistic.

Mark Martin's definition similarly endorses subjective well-being as happiness, but with the addition of "loving one's life and valuing it" and "a deep sense of meaning".[19] As we will discuss in detail, subjective well-being has philosophical hedonism at its core. Arguably, it may even be pure hedonism. This means that Martin's definition of happiness, at least partly, is philosophical hedonism. However, if "loving one's life and valuing it" and "a deep sense of meaning" are musts for a happy life, then the majority of the world's population do not qualify as happy at all, making Martin's definition of happiness idealistic as well.

Subjective well-being

A review of happiness definitions without a proper discussion on subjective well-being would be incomplete to say the least. The main body of research about happiness during the past few decades in philosophy (and to a larger extent economics, psychology, and other areas concerned with happiness and social progress) has predominantly focused on the concept of subjective well-being.[10;11] Its influence has reached far beyond the realms of philosophy, and even beyond academia. Some governments of major developed countries in the West have commissioned expert groups to find appropriate ways to measure and evaluate subjective well-being in the hope of applying it to their policies.[18]

Pioneers of subjective well-being W. Wilson[8] and Diener et al[9] quoted Dodge's writings of the 1930s, which argued that "theories of happiness [have] not advanced beyond those formulated by the Greek philosophers".[9] In saying this, the authors implied (perhaps unconsciously) that the concept of subjective well-being represents progress in the search for and exploration of the mystery of happiness.

So what is subjective well-being? Wilson's definition is "avowed happiness", in other words, whatever people deemed happiness to be.[8] In Diener et al's components of subjective well-being,[9] it includes pleasant effects (joy, elation, contentment, pride, affection, happiness, ecstasy), less un-pleasant effects (guilt and shame, sadness, anxiety and worry, anger, stress, depression, envy), life satisfaction (desire to change life, satisfaction with current life, satisfaction with past, satisfaction with future, significant other's views of one's life), and domain satisfaction (work, family, leisure, health, finances, self, one's group).

At a glance, subjective well-being attempts to include every conceivable positive: matters, states, emotion, phenomena, and evaluation — everything that people experience or evaluate in life. As pointed out by Diener et al, it's not a monolithic entity, rather a mixture of separable components that correlate and overlap in a reciprocal cause-and-effect relationship.[9] Because of this, one researcher's subjective well-being (such as positive emotions) is different from another's (such as satisfaction in work). In the components listed by Diener et al, happiness is relegated to pleasures in this hotchpotch of positivity.[9] To confuse matters, research papers about subjective well-being, including those by Diener et al, often use the term interchangeably with "happiness".

The predominant methods of subjective well-being research rely on cross-sectional surveys to provide correlational analysis between subjective well-being and its correlates.[9] The most-used (and in the author's opinion, the best in its approximation to happiness) is global self-reported happiness or life satisfaction.[9] A typical question in a survey of global happiness is "Taking all things together, how happy are you?" The answers range from 0–10 (sometimes from 0–7, depending on the survey design) where 0 means extremely unhappy and 10 means extremely happy. Similarly, in a survey of global life satisfaction, a question will be something like "All things considered, how satisfied are you with your life overall?"

Theoretically, subjective well-being includes all of the components listed previously, as quoted by Diener et al.[9] However, in the actual measurement of such surveys, the results are almost entirely a self-reported self-evaluation of life. Therefore, the definition of happiness or life satisfaction in subjective well-being is up to the individuals surveyed, as precisely described by Wilson's avowed happiness.[8] The concept of happiness in the minds of the vast majority of the general population is philosophical hedonism to say the least. Thus, philosophically, subjective well-being is philosophical hedonism or even pure hedonism. If subjective well-being is regarded as progress in our understanding of happiness, then Socrates, Plato, Aristotle, or even Epicurus would not be happy with this progress, at least from a philosophical standpoint.

However, progress is being made in the development of subjective well-being, not in its philosophical aspect but in its success at quantifying (or at least its attempt to quantify) happiness. Although the quality of methods and measurements of subjective well-being are still far from ideal (as admitted by even its most faithful supporters[11;9]), they have greatly advanced over previous efforts in quantifying the measurement of subjective well-being. This means that statistical analysis of relationships between happiness and all of its correlates is now possible.

Bentham proposed "felicific calculus" to add all pleasures (minus pains) together in the measurement of utility, but he made no progress further than merely tabulating pleasures. The real progress of subjective well-being, in the author's opinion, is not philosophical progress in the concept of happiness, but its success in making Bentham's felicific calculus a reality, even if only in a primal version. The concept of subjective well-being is much closer to Bentham's utility than Socrates' happiness. So, while Socrates would most likely frown on subjective well-being, Bentham must be smiling in heaven.

In summary, as with ordinary people, philosophers seem having difficult in agreeing on what happiness is. Depending on whether pleasures are accepted as happiness (or some kinds of happiness) or not, happiness definitions can be classified into two main categories: philosophical hedonistic or idealistic. In ancient and earlier times, happiness was regarded higher and more idealistic as Socrates' ultimate human desire and Aristotle's human Telos. On the other end, pleasures are accepted as happiness as in today's mainstream understanding of happiness such as subjective well-being, though reluctantly by some.

CHAPTER 2:

Happiness Is Experienced — Life Dissected

Happiness is about life, human life. The term "human life" has two main meanings: life as an organism and life as a process. Human life as an organism means a human being with a physical body and mental or psychological components. Biology and medical sciences are concerned with studying the physical aspects of a human; psychology and psychiatry with the mental aspects. The process of life is defined as the moment a human is born to the moment they die. The average human currently has a lifespan of about 70 years, meaning a process of around 25,550 days. Happiness is about human life *as a process*. It's about what a person experiences during those 25,550 days. All human lives, whether great human beings such as sages and heroes or "common" and "ordinary" people like the vast majority of us, have to live their entire life from moment to moment without exception. Happiness is about how people experience things from moment to moment throughout their individual life processes.

All life experiences are present. Nobody can live in the past or the future. We can experience the past in our memory and the future in our imagination and wishful thinking, but only in the present moment. We can experience childhood joy in our memory only through retrieving and bringing our memories of it to our present consciousness. When we imagine something like a holiday we'll take in the future, in the present moment, it is merely imagination. From one moment to the next, all human life is experienced in the present.

Terms relating to happiness

Happiness is about life experiences and life experiences only. Contrary to Martin's claims that the meaning of happiness has different implications in various languages[19], the meaning of happiness in the everyday language of diverse countries is quite clear.[9] Multiple research has found that people understand and answer consistently when asked whether they are happy or not.[9] In all languages, the words used about happiness in daily life, such as a happy event, a happy person, happy birthday, happy new year, happy couple, happy mood, and happy personality, are understood and used clearly by ordinary people. The terms relating and referring to happiness all point to the same base: a happy life experience.

For example, "happy birthday!" is perhaps the most often-heard utterance to a family member or friend on their birthday. We understand when we say "happy birthday!" to someone that we're wishing for them to be happy and to experience happiness during perhaps the most important day of their year. Their parents and friends might celebrate the day with them to let the person feel special, with the hope that they can feel and experience happiness even if just on this day. The day in question could be sunny, cloudy, rainy, or cold, but a "happy birthday" wish means nothing other than for its recipient to experience happiness on this day.

Similarly, we salute each other on New Year's Eve with "Happy New Year!" to wish each other happiness for the entirety of the coming year. The meaning of this wish is clear to everyone —to experience a lot of happiness, rather than sadness or bad luck in the coming year.

The same holds when happy is used as an adjective to describe other things or events in life. "happy hour", advertised by many bars to entice customers, only makes sense in relation to the experiences of patrons of said bar who not only enjoy drinks (a pleasure) but can also buy them at a discounted price (another pleasure). Without that implication, the "happy" in "happy hour" wouldn't make sense. "Happy hour" is neither happy nor sad to a non-drinker. To a spouse or child whose alcoholic partner or parent is getting intoxicated, "happy hour" may even be sad.

A happy event, such as the rise in stock prices or stock investments performing well (as mentioned in Martin's book[19]), makes sense only with the implication that it will make the owner of the stocks happy at the moment they become aware that their stock has risen in value. If the stock owner dies right after a rise but before they learn about it, the rise becomes irrelevant to their happiness. The happiness of the event is also subjective; to people other than the stock owner, it might have a negative effect. For example, those who sold the stock to its present owner may experience significant disappointment when they learn that its value has risen. Traders who've been shorting the stocks may also feel sadness when the price rises. To the vast majority of people in the stock market who have never owned these stocks, the price rise and its effect on the owner will be irrelevant. Thus, the "happy" event of a stock price rising has no intrinsic "happiness" value at all. It only makes sense if the stock owner learned of his gain and felt or experienced happiness as a result.

Sometimes, we describe a person who always seems to be happy as having a "happy character". But of course, there is no such thing as a happy character. A happy character refers to a person who often experiences happiness in life. The "character" of a person refers to the traits or qualities they possess, which normally remain stable throughout adult life and almost all life circumstances. For example, an extrovert is more willing to socialise in a random encounter with strangers than an introvert is. Similarly, an optimist is more likely to see the bright side of a situation than a pessimist is, even when faced with the same situation. In contrast, even very happy people will experience the same deep sadness as unhappy people when faced with a tragedy such as the death of a child.[35] Similarly, both happy and unhappy people would be joyous if they won millions on the lottery.

There are always exceptions, but almost everyone experiences happiness in their lives. The difference between happy and unhappy exists only in relation to the quantity or level of happiness.[9] Also, people with opposing characters, such as an extrovert who engages in social activities with great enthusiasm and an introvert who is quietly content with their private life, could both be happy.[9]

Similarly, we refer to a "happy couple" for no other reason than that they experience more happiness than others (on average) in their marriage. A happy couple enjoys each other's company and experience more happiness (as opposed to acrimony or apathy) in their marriage. On their wedding day, every couple looks like a happy couple. In reality, few could truly win this crown of ordinary adult life, as close to 40% of marriages end in divorce[36]. Couples who appear odd to others because of their looks, height, social status, education, or family background can all be called happy couples if they experience more happiness in their marital life than more conventional couples. In terms of happiness, it's one of life's greatest fortunes when you find your soulmate in your significant other.[37]

"I'm happy with it" is a statement we sometimes make when we agree or are satisfied with an arrangement, situation, or result. Although the arrangement, situation, or result is not an experience in itself, we feel happy (satisfied) when we have reviewed and evaluated it at the moment we make that statement. For example, when asked our opinion about a cold, wet winter (a situation), we may say "I'm happy with it so far" to express the good feeling of realising that our decision to sign up for an indoor yoga course three months ago was a wise one. Another case for stating "I'm happy with it" often occurs for students in high school or college at the end of a semester or term. Although academic learning is seldom a happy experience, they may feel satisfied (happy) at the moment the semester ends because they achieved a B in calculus, despite half the class quitting during the semester and less than half of the remainder achieving a C or above.

"Happy" is always apt for describing an experience such as happy eating, happy walking, happy networking, Happy Christmas, Happy Halloween, happy reading, etc. Even happy shitting makes great sense to people suffering from constipation!

"Happy life" is an overall evaluation of the moment-to-moment life experience of a person across their whole life, a comprehensive summary of their life so far. A happy life is not a concept defined by Martin as different from the moment-to-moment experiences of a happy person.[19] Instead, a happy life is an evaluation of life overall lived by a happy person (of course, what we mean by a happy person is relative and subjective, changing with time). A happy life can only be judged after all the days of that life are experienced and finished.

As described in Diener et al,[9] the components of subjective well-being are all experienced as positive or (less) negative effects, which are direct life experiences, as well as reviewed and evaluated experiences in life overall or in certain specific aspects of life. These are divided into global satisfaction and domain satisfactions.[38]

How we experience life: awareness

So, how do we experience our moment-to-moment life? We experience it through our awareness or our faculty (capacity) of awareness. Awareness is defined as the ability to directly know and perceive, to feel, or to be cognisant of events ... the state of being conscious of something.[39] But how do we become aware or cognisant of our life? How do we perceive, feel, or know it? I classify our faculty of awareness into four or five groups or levels of awareness that a human being normally possesses.

- First, we have awareness of our body, including the senses of our sense organs such as eyes, ears, tongue, skin, etc.

- Secondly, we have the awareness of mental senses: emotions such as fear, anger, approval, or disapproval.

- The third awareness is the sense of thinking, which is strictly the sense of the brain.

- The fourth is our moral sensibility or ethical judgement, which can be called "the ethical sense".

- In some people, although a minority of the population, a strong awareness of the transcendent meaning of life and a goal beyond personal or individual interests could be called "spiritual awareness", which is the fifth realm.

- In some rare cases, people could have awareness beyond these four or five realms, but such cases are beyond the limits of this book.

(These classifications are used purely for convenience when discussing human life experiences. They're by no means a strict description of the human psyche or mind, which is a discussion for another book.)

Level one: bodily awareness

The first realm of awareness is our bodily awareness. It is also the most familiar awareness to us—through our sense organs and overall body. We're aware of the colours of flowers by seeing them with our eyes. We're aware of the sweetness of candy through the taste buds on our tongue. We're aware of birds singing through our ears, and we're aware that a freshly-microwaved bowl of soup is hot when we touch the rim of the bowl. On a bodily level, we have more awareness than just our sense organs. We have awareness of all parts of our internal body, particularly when those parts are in trouble, such as the awareness of pain in any part of our body, be it our toe, head, or back.

Strong senses of coldness, hunger, or thirst are the most obvious examples, and we normally understand them as bodily desires or basic needs. However, our awareness is much more than the rough senses mentioned here, our reactions to the senses we experience in a given moment, or the past senses stored in our memory. For example, the simple desire and enjoyment of the Japanese food sashimi can be a result of either the unique sweetness of fine raw fish such as salmon, the unusual texture, the taste of soy sauce-flavoured spicy wasabi on a combined mouthful of rice and fish, or any combination of these.

Bodily awareness isn't simply "on" or "off"; it may involve different levels of awareness, commonly known as "sensibility". For example, some people can tell the subtle difference between two dishes that others are not aware of, thus they may be employed for their sensitive taste buds. We may say that someone has "the sensitivity of a dog" when they can discern a unique smell or flavour where others don't sense anything at all.

High sensibility is not necessarily a good thing (in the meaning of feeling good or bad) for its owner. Although someone with a keen ear for subtle sounds may, comparatively, get more enjoyment from listening to their favourite music, the same sensitivity will make them more aware of annoying background noises when others don't hear a thing. The person who enjoys every bit of sweetness in foods may equally suffer the bitterness of medicines. High sensitivity to bodily pains will almost always be bad for the person experiencing them (although high sensibility to pain may be good for their overall health). Different awareness levels of various sense organs and body parts give each of us unique bodily experiences in everyday life.

Level two: mental awareness

The second realm of awareness is mental awareness. The main content of mental awareness is emotions, both positive and negative, and taste (like or dislike) beyond our bodily senses. We are aware (or experience) mental awareness far more often than we do bodily awareness. Other than a few moments when we're hungry, thirsty, feeling cold, or in bodily pain, we're hardly aware of our physical body. Actually, we're more aware of our body through pain than through pleasure. However, we're aware of our mental conditions almost all of the time.

From the moment we open our eyes in the morning and become conscious of ourselves and the world outside, all kinds of emotions and worries may rush to our consciousness without any intentional effort on our part. We may have some residual mirth from last night at somebody else's expense, or excitement for an upcoming cup final involving the team we support. But most of the time, emotions and worries over mundane matters occupy our mind.

Our mental awareness is also wider than our bodily awareness. It seems we have far higher mental awareness than animals, be it from enjoying the aesthetic beauty of nature (as opposed to the utilities of nature, which seem to be the main awareness of other animals) to the delicate tastes of all kinds of human creations from symphonies to architecture. However, such high-intensity awareness of our mental realm is both a curse and a blessing, and probably more the former for ordinary people. A simple, animal-like mental life is a blessing considering how much humanity has suffered from the mental disturbances and illnesses caused by our heightened mental awareness.

Level three: thought awareness

The third realm of awareness is our thoughts and reasoning. I separate this realm from mental awareness for two reasons. Firstly, we have greater control over our thoughts than our emotions, which are more our reactions to external or internal stimuli, where the thinking process is more within our control, although we cannot have absolute control for any extended period. Secondly, emotions seem to involve other organs, particularly the heart, whereas thinking or thoughts are more strictly products of the brain and therefore are less involved with other parts of the body.

As in the previous two realms, awareness in this realm can be both a blessing and a curse. Fun childhood memories of our hometown will evoke a warm nostalgia that accompanies us for life, and the thought of opening Christmas presents is sometimes more exciting than the actual process. On the other hand, bad memories of suffering from childhood abuse can cause nightmares for many years. Also problematic is the "monkey mind" that runs wild, causing many problems for humans, particularly in this modern "information age".

Level four: ethical awareness

The fourth realm is our ethical awareness. Ethical awareness exists in almost every human being, although most people confuse their ethical awareness with their mental awareness or thoughts. Outside the religious realm, ethical awareness occurs to us clearly on certain occasions where it cannot be confused with other realms of awareness. One such occasion can be observed by ordinary people in daily life, and it clearly demonstrates the existence of human awareness in this realm — ordinary people jumping into water to save a drowning child they've never met, without any consideration for their own interest or even safety. It seems instinctive because people perform such heroic acts without any thinking process.

From my observation, this is one of the biggest differences between humans and other animals. Why humans behave so differently from other animals regarding their ability to perform instant and automatic altruistic behaviors is fascinating. At the same time, it's sobering to admit that humanity is also a species that is capable of and has committed acts far more evil than pure animal brutality. For example, even the meanest animal doesn't elicit pleasure in torturing his own kind — a common practice throughout human history. Why this is the case is still a mystery deserving serious philosophical explanation, but it's beyond the limits of this book.

When we make a moral judgement without any personal attachments, we are experiencing ethical awareness or what Jonathan Haidt defined as "a moral dimension" or "divinity", without any connotation of religion.[40] Similarly, Kant's definition of duty is moral judgement without personal attachment (personal gains or losses, like or dislike).[41] Hume's moral sentiments also describe this part of human awareness.[42] Freud's "Super-Ego" in his trilogy of human psychology: (Id, Ego, and Super-Ego) points to the part of our psyche responsible for our awareness in the ethical dimension.

Another case in recent human history demonstrates humanity's capacity in this dimension of awareness, and shows that it is clearly different from desires with a self-centered interest. Oscar Schindler and many like him risked their own lives to rescue and hide Jewish strangers from the Nazis, and in doing so, they were acting out of ethical awareness. Such actions would not provide them with any material or social gains, and they had much to lose if the Nazis caught them. In many cases, high-ranking diplomats and officials had to defy their own government policies or forge documents to save Jews. However, they knew by their intuition that their actions were right and what they ought to do. That decision made from intuition and with conviction comes from ethical awareness.

It must be pointed out here that the existence of the fourth realm of awareness, the moral dimension, does not necessarily mean that morality is founded on human sentiments, as advocated by Hume.[42] Nor is how and why humanity has this dimension of awareness a subject that we will discuss here (i.e. Freud's question of nature vs. nurture). It's an empirical phenomenon observed in various societies that we have this aspect of awareness — of right vs. wrong — although it is not absolutely universal (some have little awareness in this realm and live their lives like beasts or even worse and more commonly are confused or possessed by hatred and act more evil than beasts do). As such, the strength of awareness in this realm varies greatly from one individual to another. The ethical level of awareness is not as common as any other level of awareness discussed, which exist among almost all of humanity.

The human awareness described here is very similar to "consciousness" as defined in philosophy or psychology, and in most cases the two terms are interchangeable. However, there is a difference between them that is worth emphasising. The groups of human awareness discussed here mainly focus on experiencing aspects of the process of human life, whilst consciousness mainly focuses on the *psychological* component (the human psyche) of a human being. For example, sub-consciousness is a crucial part of the human psyche that exists and affects our mental life profoundly. But there is no sub-awareness in the other groups. This is because in experience, there are aspects of awareness that you are either aware of or not. When you're aware of something, it becomes part of your experience. When you're not aware of something, it's irrelevant to your experience. Thus, sub-consciousness may exist in our psyche all of the time. It affects us and becomes our experience only when the conscious process makes us aware of it.

Multiple levels of awareness

The idea of human beings having multiple levels of awareness of the kind discussed here has some similarity to Maslow's hierarchy or pyramid of needs.[43] There are, however, fundamental differences. The main difference is that Maslow's hierarchy or pyramid of needs focuses

[37]

mainly on the underlying motivations or desires of people's behaviors. Whereas the multiple levels of awareness discussed here focus on the awareness or the experiences we are conscious of at any given moment. Awareness accompanies us from moment to moment when we are conscious, but desires do not. Desires (motivation) are only part of our awareness in its entirety when experienced in every moment of a day.

For example, when we open our eyes in the morning, we are aware of our bedroom, the condition of our partner (still sleeping or awake), and the hungry feeling of our stomach. The awareness of hunger will result in the desire to eat breakfast, but the awareness of our bedroom, the furniture, and the lights is so familiar to us that we're barely aware of them, so they won't create any desires inside us. When we open our bedroom curtains, we may be aware of the sunshine, a stormy blizzard, or a regular cloudy morning. The awareness of sunny weather and that today is Sunday may create a desire to stroll around the lake after breakfast. The awareness of stormy weather and that today is Sunday will probably not create the same desire, but instead create the desire to stay in and read a book. The awareness of sunny weather on what happens to be a work day probably won't create the desire to take a walk around the lake either, but create a feeling of pity that we have to go to work instead of taking a leisurely morning stroll. Thus, awareness seems more fundamental to desires and the roots of our desires. What awareness is and its relationship to human needs or desires is beyond the limits of this book and deserves a whole book in its own right.

Awareness is richer in its contents than the needs and wants of an individual. The simple desire and decision to eat Greek salad instead of a tasty cheeseburger for lunch may come from a pure preference for Greek salad over a cheeseburger, taste awareness, health considerations (the awareness that vegetables are better for health), or ethical considerations (the awareness that it's wrong to kill animals for food when we have alternative ways of feeding ourselves).

Awareness is also wider in scope than the needs and wants of an individual. Most of the time, we have no strong intentions or desires to do anything, and we don't know what to do with ourselves (a boring Sunday afternoon, for example). But when awake, we have constant awareness. We even have awareness when we are dreaming, sometimes vividly remembering the scenes and episodes of our dreams afterwards. Surprises in life are awareness involving experience outside our desires or expectations (needs or wants). Bumping into an old friend we lost contact with long ago is a typical surprise that was not part of our expectations. It's precisely the very unlikely occurrence of meeting our old friend that makes it so exceptional in the joy it creates for us and the excitement we experience in the moment we meet them. One of the delights of nature is that there may be a surprise lurking anywhere and at any moment. The observation of and encounters with surprises are experiences outside the realms of our needs or wants but are part of our experience through awareness.

It's not just surprises that are outside our desires (needs and wants) but part of our everyday experience of life. Many things we experience in life that we deem beyond our ability to change are regarded as "natural"; we seldom have any expectations of them. For example, few people pay attention to how the sun rises every day because it's such a regular, monotonous phenomenon. But one day, you may be delighted to find the sun rising from the east with intense fire and brightness. Perhaps some more common things about the sun bring us pleasure. When you're gardening under a spring sun, the warmth of the gentle sunlight gives you a nice sensation beyond your expectations — sunny, overcast, or rain being our typical expectations of spring.

There are other unchangeable things in life also treated as natural and often outside our desires or expectations. For example, most people regard their own temper or personality as "the way life is", whether one likes it or not. The ageing process, with its grey hairs, wrinkles, aches, and pains is also regarded as natural in most people's minds — we would be suspicious of someone who seriously expected to remain young forever. These issues, along with our mental and physical health conditions, severely affect the quality of our life — or our awareness of pain or happiness — but are often outside the realm of our expectations or desires because they're regarded as "the way it is". You have to accept these things as they are, no matter how painful they are (think of chronic conditions such as severe arthritis).

Another important difference between Maslow's hierarchy or pyramid of needs and the concept of multiple human awareness suggested here is that Maslow's human needs have a hierarchy[43], whereas the concept of multiple human awareness does not. From the large base of physiological needs to the top of self-realisation, Maslow's human needs are pyramid-shaped. Maslow's theory suggests that the most basic level of needs must be met before the individual will strongly desire (or focus their motivation on) the secondary, or higher-level, needs. However, with multiple levels of human awareness, there is no hierarchy in which level(s) of our awareness will be dominant in our consciousness at any given moment. In human awareness, it seems that the strongest signal from any or all levels of our awareness, either positive (good feeling) or negative (bad feeling), will be take the centre stage of our conscious mind. Interestingly, with human desires, we always desire something good, from basic physiological needs to the top of self-realisation. However, in human awareness, we are more aware of "bad awareness" than "good awareness" in our everyday life and as this book argues, it's the bad awareness (fetters, which you will learn more about in the next chapter) that play a key role in human happiness.

In conclusion

Multiple levels of human awareness are wider in range and richer in content than Maslow's multiple levels of human needs. Human awareness is probably the most essential aspect of human life because without awareness, we would be in a persistent vegetative state in a hospital bed. Human awareness is probably more fundamental than human desires (motivation), and may even be the foundation for human desires.

So, it begs the question, how do we experience our life overall with the four or five realms of awareness? It's like having a four– or five–member tribunal deciding what we're going to experience at any given moment. The members of the tribunal are the levels of our awareness, and they are constantly competing with each other to have their say. The "opinions" of these members on the tribunal panel are not fixed or even stable at any particular moment. Each realm of awareness is in itself a dynamic flux that is in an almost-constant state of change.

To complicate matters, the tribunal member who will win the competition to have their say are as mysterious as anything could be on this planet. There's no fixed pattern for people in general or particular, but neither is it totally random. Sometimes, we (the concise mind) have our say when we pay special attention to something. But most of the time, we are almost as passive and powerless as passengers on a wild vehicle ride, being driven simultaneously by four or five unruly drivers on an open African savannah.

We have multiple levels of awareness at all times in our everyday life. We experience our life from moment to moment through all of the faculties of our awareness. Sometimes, we focus on only one aspect of our awareness — concentrating all of our attention on the smell or taste of wine when asked to approve a bottle in a restaurant or immersing ourselves in our favourite music. Most of the time, however, we experience life from moment to moment with a dynamic flux of multiple levels of awareness.

At any given moment, we may experience multiple levels of awareness simultaneously. For example, when you're having lunch with a friend, you can maintain a conversation while eating. At the same moment, you may notice a new outfit your friend is wearing and become jealous of how their fashionable clothes make yours look bland. All of these and much more may happen simultaneously, alternately, or randomly in our conscious mind during one lunch meeting. Focusing on, or being aware of, only one level of our awareness is much less common than there being a constant whirlpool of dramas, emotions, and thoughts happening inside us as we live our ordinary lives. When the pleasant feeling — the positive side of experience — wins the argument in the tribunal and dominates our awareness, we feel happiness at that moment of our life.

CHAPTER 3:

Happiness: The Definition

Happiness is a state we are aware of or we feel. It is a state of freedom, more specifically a state of freedom from fetters, which are inevitable parts of human life. To understand the hypothesis of happiness proposed here, we must first clarify a couple of concepts used in the previous statement, namely "freedom" and "fetters".

What are fetters?

The term "freedom" has two main meanings. The first is the privilege to choose, for instance, political freedom (the right to choose from candidates for government), freedom of religion (the right to choose a faith), or freedom of speech (the right to speak one's mind). The second is a lack of confinement, such as prison, or an escape from harm (such as persecution) or relief from burdens (such as a mortgage i.e. financial freedom).

The first is usually a choice among "good" things and is expressed as the freedom "of" things such as expression of one's mind, whereas the second is more often related to "bad" things that people try to avoid or escape, and is often expressed as the freedom "from" things, such as prison, persecution, illnesses, burdens, etc.

The definition of freedom in the hypothesis of happiness used in this book takes the second meaning of freedom: freedom from bad things, emancipation from restrictions that make us uncomfortable or cause us pain. The freedom of good things and freedom from bad things I describe here is similar to the positive and negative freedoms articulated by Isaiah Berlin[44], although I have expanded "bad" things to cover a much wider range than the external coercions used in classical discussions of liberty.

The term "fetters" I have used here needs more explanation and is a key to understanding the concept and definition of happiness in this book.

"Fetter" is an old English word and its frequency in use is in decline, perhaps even obsolete. The word's original meaning is pretty simple: a chain or shackle placed on the feet. It is usually used as a plural, fetters, to mean anything that confines or restrains, and can be both a noun and a verb. I have taken the liberty of expanding the traditional meaning in this book so I can define and explain my hypothesis of happiness clearly and concisely.

The term fetter, or fetters, I use here to represent anything that causes pain, discomfort, hurt, disappointment, concern, worry, shock, anger, stress, sorrow, anxiety, regret, guilt, self-doubt, or something that is burdensome, overwhelming, tiring, unpleasant, or uneasy, or that causes painful feelings or sensations that we would normally try to avoid.

In chapter one, I called subjective well-being a hotchpotch of positivity. Fetters, as defined here and used throughout this book, can be considered subjective *not*-well-being, a hotchpotch of negativity. Thus, fetters are the opposite of subjective well-being. When we become aware of fetters, we lose the nice feeling of subjective well-being. People often use other names such as pains, baggage, burdens, bonds, uneasiness, or sufferings for anything that causes them pain or discomfort.

While these terms have similar meanings to fetters as defined here, their conventional meanings are not wide or precise enough to cover all of the cases I include in my definition of fetters. For example, pain or suffering normally means the physical ailments or mental torment that are the main parts of human not-well-being. However, a lot of other things can cause us discomfort in life, such as the loss of quiet enjoyment and privacy that a person may experience when they become famous. In this case, it is a little far-fetched to define fame as pain or suffering, but appropriate to say that fame can become a fetter to people with regards to quiet enjoyment and privacy. The closest everyday words to fetters are "troubles" or "problems". Yet the trouble and problem with troubles and problems is that they're too common and too widely used in literature and daily language. Using them as synonyms for the specific meaning of fetters in this book could cause confusion. Again, fetters as used throughout this book means anything that causes unpleasant, uneasy, or painful feelings or sensations in one or more realms of our awareness. Happiness, therefore, is a state when our awareness is free from fetters – free from bad things.

What are fetters in our levels of awareness?

As discussed at the end of the last chapter, we experience every moment of our life through a dynamic combined process of multiple levels of awareness, a tribunal panel of four or five members. Each panel member has its own characters or traits that change through time. What each level of our awareness contains in terms of components, contents, and intensities is unique to each individual. We can feel or be aware of each level of our awareness from the best (highest) end to the worst (lowest) end and everywhere between.

For example, through the awareness of our taste buds, we can experience both the delicious taste of gourmet food at our favourite restaurant and the most disgusting medicine we ever had to take. It's most likely that we taste our everyday meals or snacks somewhere between these two extremes. When not eating or drinking, we will seldom be aware of our taste buds unless we have a problem with our digestive system, which may cause uncomfortable and unusual tastes in the mouth.

At a bodily level of awareness, in addition to the taste buds on the tongue, we have awareness through our sense organs: eyes, ears, nose, and skin. However, bodily awareness is not only limited to sense organs. We have awareness of the conditions in our internal body (every part of the body not belonging to any particular sense organ).

We feel energetic and fresh after a good and deep sleep. We feel tired but warm and relaxed after a hot shower at the end of a long day. We have bad (negative) feelings about our body as well. In fact, aches and pains are the aspects of our bodies that we're most aware of in our adult life. Exceptionally few adults could enjoy ideal bodily health without any common aches, such as back or neck pains. These are commonly known as pains of our physical body and are among the main fetters that cause unhappiness to ordinary people. In any given moment, we can be conscious of feelings or sensations from the best to the worst — with any awareness of our body from sense organs or from the internal senses of any part of our body.

We experience three or four groups of awareness in a similar way to how we experience bodily awareness. There is a wide spectrum of experiences for each group of awareness, from the best to the worst we have ever experienced. For example, when it comes to a given aspect of our life (such as our ability to handle problems at work) we can on an emotional level experience anything from full confidence and self-esteem to despondence, depression, and everything in between. Similarly, in the realm of thought awareness, we may experience everything from the fond memory of our team winning a critical match the previous night to self-loathing about our failure in controlling our emotions whilst watching the game, and everything in between. In the ethical realm of our awareness, we can experience everything from the peaceful inner feeling of doing the morally right thing (even if it means sacrificing our self-interest) to deep feelings of guilt and regret when we know we've done something morally wrong.

What is happiness?

Happiness is a state or experience we are aware of or feel. It is a state of freedom, specifically from fetters. At any given moment in our life, when the fetters in all levels of our awareness are blocked out of our consciousness, then we feel (experience) happiness at that precious moment of being trouble-free and worry-free. In other words, happiness is the time when our consciousness is free from fetters. The happiness definitions we discussed in the first chapter differ only in their degree or duration of freedom from fetters.

All of the given definitions of happiness have one common denominator: a state where our awareness is free from fetters, whether it's a short moment of relaxation and gratification when sipping our favourite beer at a local bar or a long-lasting worry-free trouble-free life in heaven. The different definitions of happiness we reviewed in chapter 1 differ only in their specific conditions that result in freedom from fetters. Thus, freedom from fetters underlies *all* definitions of happiness.

Pleasures are temporary reliefs that free us from fetters, or more accurately that temporarily mask fetters from our conscious mind. Pleasures such as eating a favourite cookie, drinking a glass of cold water after a hard workout, enjoying a soccer game, or having spiritual feelings in a grand cathedral are merely states of freedom from our fetters at different levels, for different durations.

Human beings, even the lucky few who live in the democratic societies of developed countries, are not truly free as they are chained to, shackled with, or bonded to all kinds of fetters. Fetters can appear in many different ways, such as a shortage of food when hungry, a lack of drinking water when thirsty, not enough clothing on a cold day, or noises that keep us awake all night.

One common trait among fetters is that they all cause us pain or suffering. When we experience a moment of freedom from the grip of these fetters, we have that worry-and-pain-free feeling of happiness. That moment is most often created when we are doing something fun, interesting, or pleasurable. At that moment, the conscious feeling of pain and suffering is absent from our mind, and we simply forget about our fetters for a while. Unfortunately, as human beings, we are tied so tightly to so many fetters that our moments of freedom from them always seems short and fleeting. This is why, in ordinary human lives, happiness is always elusive and short, but pain and suffering is obvious and lasting. Moreover, this is what Buddhism means when it asserts that "human life is suffering".

Happiness is a state when our mind's attention is away from ourselves. The main reason for this is that our internal fetters (mental fetters and chaotic thoughts) are almost omnipresent when we are awake. Any self-centred attention will automatically bring these fetters into our consciousness. We will automatically be aware of all the pain, worries, and shortcomings we have at the time, things that cause suffering by their very nature. Therefore, short-lived pleasures are fleeting moments when our attention is away from ourselves, as there is a positive outside stimulus strong enough to attract our attention. Flow, which is claimed as the optimal human experience[13], is a long period when we focus our attention on something very interesting, totally forgetting our worries and self-consciousness in the process. Therefore, Flow is a prolonged or extended pleasure.

What is pleasure?

Pleasure is temporary relief from our awareness (or consciousness) of fetters. The feeling of pleasure is created at the moment that our fetters are kept from entering our mind or feelings, freeing us from their grip. This feeling happens when our desire resonates with an outside stimulus or internal thought. At that moment, the pleasant vibration dominates our consciousness, which is otherwise always dealing with unpleasant feelings or chaotic conditions. As you saw in chapter 2, happiness is experienced life dissected. At any given moment, our consciousness is a dynamic, fluid competition or a tug of war between the positive and negative on four to five levels of awareness. When the positive awareness is winning the tug of war or is dominant in the dynamic, fluid equilibrium, we feel pleasure as we forget about our troubles (fetters) in life.

There are so many ways to obtain pleasure that categorising them *a la* Bentham is exhausting. It seems like we all know what can bring us fun and pleasure, even if the things that give us pleasure can be amazingly different. The food we eat, the clothes we wear, the way we decorate our home, the way we spend our weekend... these all reflect the vast, diverse spectrum of human interests and preferences.

Who doesn't know the little pleasures in life? A favourite cookie, a new toy, a dazzling display of spring bulbs in blossom, an unexpected pay rise, a favourite video game, a surprise encounter with an old friend... the list is endless. Moreover, trades and businesses of all kinds exist, survive, and thrive in delivering products or services that bring pleasure to their clients.

Aristotle said that pleasure is in activities. However, as humans cannot carry out continuous activities all of the time, then we cannot be happy all the time. Aristotle was right that when we are in action, we feel pleasure. However, even Aristotle, one of the greatest philosophers humanity has to offer, was misled in believing that the activity *itself* provides the pleasure, as were other prominent thinkers such as Jeremy Bentham and John Stuart Mill. Aristotle failed to realise that pleasure is only a trick to hide the dark side of being a human, which is constantly suffering from the fetters that chain us so tightly in our everyday lives. The pleasure itself, or more accurately, the activities that bring us pleasurable feelings, cannot do the trick alone. Pleasurable activities can bring us pleasure *only if* the activity absorbs our attention enough to block the fetters from our conscious mind or our awareness.

Case study: Killer whales vs. seasickness

The enlightening moment for me, the realisation of the essence of pleasures, came when I observed first-hand what happened to my son on a whale-watching tour.

At the time, my son was nine. Full of energy and curiosity at a world so full of fun, there wasn't a moment when he didn't have a smile on his face. He was always fond of animals. Aged two, he'd been awed and fascinated by the size and unreal beauty of a killer whale when he first saw one at the Stanley Park Aquarium in Vancouver, Canada. Now, on a summer morning in Tofino, Vancouver Island, he was excited and anxious to be out in the sea, watching killer whales in the wild, their natural home. But contrary to his expectations, the tour was a nightmare for him. I had never seen him suffer so much in the whole of his young life. He was severely seasick. Not long after we boarded the small boat and started from Tofino dock, he started feeling dizzy and developed a headache. The further we went out to sea, and the higher the waves got, the worse his condition became. I sat right beside him the whole time, lending my shoulder for support and comforting him as best I could. I tried to divert his attention from his headache and stomach pains by pointing out interesting wild animals we saw along the way, such as birds, otters, and sea lions. But nothing, even the excitement of the whole boat when we saw a pod of killer whales, seemed to alleviate his suffering. His only reaction was to raise his head for a couple of seconds. He constantly asked, "When will we go back?" It seemed like an eternity for both of us. Sighting a rare wild animal as big as a whale would be really exciting for him under normal circumstances, but it did not materialise during that whale-watching tour. It had nothing to do with the sighting of the whales itself — the problem was his seasickness, which was the fetter that brought him such unbearable suffering. The suffering of being seasick was so strong and overwhelming that nothing could mask it from his bodily awareness, conscious feeling, or mind. Neither his favourite candy nor the biggest animal in the wild could divert his attention from the dizziness or nausea. The only thing on his mind was jumping from the damn boat onto solid earth, escaping from the hell of the sea and the boat.

You see, pleasure only masks our fetters. This can explain why people who are mentally ill barely experience pleasure in their lives. Psychiatrists have explained that schizophrenics suffer from **anhedonia**, the inability to feel pleasure.[45] Schizophrenia is caused by excessive stimuli. There are so many things and so much going on in the head of someone with schizophrenia that almost nothing can mask or block the stimuli from their consciousness, even for a fleeting moment. These stimuli are strong, chaotic, uncontrollable thoughts and the negative emotions of anger, sadness, fear, worry, and anxiety — all painful fetters. Many of the perceived "dubious" behaviours of mentally ill people are desperate attempts to mask or escape the unbearable pain of intense mental fetters.

The things that bring pleasure to non-mentally-ill people, such as watching a movie, playing a game, or having a conversation with a friend, cannot block the extreme mental fetters from the minds of those with mental illness, so these activities will not bring them pleasure at all. Alcohol, drugs, and all types of substances are used to alleviate these fetters, even for just one pain-free moment of refuge. The assault of severe mental illness is so bad that even self-inflicted physical pain is used as a relief.[46] When the negative side of life, the fetters, are so many and so strong, barely anything can block these fetters from the mind. This explains why those who are mentally ill or severely disturbed seldom feel happy in life.

Why do mentally ill people self-inflict bodily pain?

For some people who are suffering severe mental anguish, even physical pains are intentionally applied — self-harm — to relieve the more unbearable mental pains. This is unexplainable with any understanding of pleasures and pains that regards them as separate, unrelated events. With such understanding, it makes no sense for the severely mentally ill to add physical pains onto their mental anguish as it will double their pains. However, with the mechanism of the happiness hypothesis proposed in this book, it is both rational and understandable that a person might inflict physical pain to block the mental anguishes that are far worse.

When the conscious mind is occupied by physical pain, the person is freed from the more dreadful mental anguish. In such cases, physical pain provides the mentally ill person with temporary, partial freedom from the worst part of fetters (mental anguish) and offer a better condition than that of no physical pain (though as physical pains are still fetters, it is not a pleasurable experience).

Most people would not use physical pain to deviate mental pain intentionally, but we do experience similar "benefits" when one pain (or fetter) blocks another. We often suffer multiple troubles and problems in our daily life. When our minds are totally occupied by one prominent concern, we feel less bothered by our other problems. As soon as the most prominent problem is solved, however, the next most prominent problem in the queue will immediately become our main concern.

The understanding of pleasure as a way of pushing fetters out of our minds can explain a lot of phenomena we experience or observe in our daily life. For example, children of every generation, at all levels of society, in any given country, regardless of their family's income seem to experience more fun and pleasure than adults from the same family. The reason for this may be that children have far fewer fetters in their life — and with their innate strong curiosity, what might seem trivial to an adult can absorb a child's attention and bring them fun and pleasure for hours. Children experience a lot of Flow,[13] often without many material possessions such as toys. It is not uncommon for children to play with their friends for a whole day using just mud or play hide-and-seek for hours on end.

Another experience we have all encountered in our daily life is the varying degree of pleasure that different things bring us. Our level of enjoyment depends on how much and how long an activity blocks our fetters from our awareness. Drinking a morning coffee is often part of a daily routine, which is a fetter to us, rather than a true enjoyment. The habitual act is the main driver for us to drink that must-have coffee, with little enjoyment for the aroma of the coffee itself. More often than not, we don't pay much attention to the taste or fragrance of the coffee. Our attention is still on whatever's occupying our mind at the time.

On the other hand, when we are doing our favourite things in our life — Flow activities such as playing a beloved ball games with our buddies — our attention is completely focused on the game and everything else is blocked from our consciousness. All of the worries, anxieties, sadness, anger, and longings in our life are suspended or forgotten, at least for the moment we are playing the ball game, in that precious moment of pain-free, worry-free happiness.[13]

One final case demonstrates that pleasurable feelings are created by the absorption of our attention in an activity — and it is the pleasure of reading. Reading can be quite pleasurable but difficult to explain through conventional ways of understanding pleasure, because the act of reading does not at any given moment provide an intensive feeling, unlike other typical pleasure activities such as drinking or eating. The key to finding pleasure or fun in reading is always the intensive interest in the material we are reading, not the importance of the material or the benefit we may obtain from reading it. It's our absorbing interest in the stories we're reading that performs the trick of blocking our fetters from our awareness. To most people, therefore, books that are filled with stories they find the most fascinating are their favourites.

The different forms (experiences) of happiness described in the happiness definitions in chapter 1 are all fundamentally freedom from fetters but to different degrees. Most of the pleasures we experience in everyday life offer only partial freedom, while the ideal happiness proposed in various idealistic definitions means *complete* freedom from fetters. Ordinary pleasures are only partial or incomplete freedom from fetters.

The incompleteness of freedom from fetters in ordinary pleasures is two-fold. Firstly, most pleasures are not deep (or intensive) enough to block out all fetters across the four or five levels of our awareness. The depth or intensity of our pleasure depends on how strong the stimulus is, as well as the level of our interest (desire) in the activity. For example, an unexpected Christmas bonus is a delight but quite a different experience from winning the lottery, which could cause euphoria at the moment of winning. As with our interest in an activity, the stronger our desire, the stronger our pleasure will be.

Secondly, most pleasures are short-lived, sometimes being little more than a fleeting sense. This is what Buddhists are talking about when they say that "life is suffering". All pleasures are merely the moment when our awareness is occupied by the resonation of our desires with external or internal stimuli. When — and only when — that resonation is strong enough to block all of our fetters from our awareness do we feel that moment of freedom, which is the feeling of pleasure or happiness. Unfortunately, the resonation of our desires with stimuli are quite short, a fleeting moment in the vast majority of pleasures in our daily life. The rest of the time, we're mostly in a state of being aware or conscious of some negative feelings or chaotic thoughts, which are all fetters in our lives.

The main reason why all idealists dismiss pleasure in their definition of happiness is because it offers only *partial* freedom from fetters. Think back to a few of the idealists' quotes from chapter 1.

Rousseau: "Even in our keenest pleasures there is scarcely a single moment of which the heart could truthfully say: 'Would that this moment could last forever!' How can we give the name of happiness to a fleeting state which leaves our hearts still empty and anxious, either regretting something that is past or desiring something that is yet to come?"[29]

Ricard: "Happiness can't be limited to a few pleasant sensations, to some intense pleasure, to an eruption of joy or a fleeting sense of serenity, to a cherry day or a magic moment that sneaks upon us in the labyrinth of our existence. Such diverse facets are not enough in themselves to build an accurate image of the profound and lasting fulfilment that characterizes true happiness." [32]

St Augustine: "Happiness is fullness or plenitude flowing in such a way that the one who experiences it lacks nothing, knows no want. Those who are happy are not in need but are filled with the supreme measure of wisdom. To be happy is thus to be suffused with truth, to have God within the soul, to enjoy God."[22]

Thus, due to the incompleteness of freedom from fetters in all levels of awareness, pleasures in the daily lives of ordinary people will always leave them feeling that something missing and that they are still longing for something better.

I argue in this hypothesis that happiness is the ultimate freedom for humanity. In classical understandings of the concept of freedom or liberty, it mainly concerns "free will" and coercion in social life, particularly in the realm of organisation and governance of societies.[47,48] Therefore, the freedom (liberty), both positive and negative, as articulated by Isaiah Berlin[44] is limited to issues of interpersonal coercion and burdens (fetters). In the wider realm, Stoics, ascetics, and spiritual seekers expanded human freedom to mean emancipation from our own desires and mental disturbance (particularly anxiety).[49,50]

The ultimate freedom I articulate here is freedom from *all* restrictions (troubles, burdens, or fetters) placed on humanity when we live on earth (this book does not discuss life after death). The restrictions (troubles, burdens, or fetters) include not only coercion and encroachment in political, social, or interpersonal realms; desires or mental disturbance in internal mental realms; but all troubles and problems (fetters) that we experience in our four or five levels of awareness. Pain, suffering from illness (including diseases), poverty, and lack of opportunity for self-realisation are also included as fetters that we must be freed from to reach the ultimate freedom as humans.

With the ultimate freedom, we not only want to liberate ourselves from coercion by others, and our internal desires and mental disturbances, but also shackles such as illness, disasters, and disabilities placed on us by nature, inheritance, or fate. It was wise for the founding fathers of the United States to place "pursuing happiness" in the Constitution instead of happiness itself because happiness, the ultimate freedom for humans, is beyond any government's capability to bestow on their citizens.

The ultimate freedom is a salvation for humans in a secular sense. When we obtain this ultimate freedom, we can live in heaven while still on earth, which Christians envisioned as only being possible after death. With this ultimate freedom in mind, we can understand why Socrates, Plato, Aristotle, Epicurus, Zeno, and many that came after them such as Rousseau all claimed that men who obtained true happiness would rival gods[5]. With this understanding of happiness as the ultimate freedom, we can truly appreciate why Socrates stated that happiness is human beings' ultimate desire[1] and Aristotle's claim that happiness is the Telos of humans.[2]

CHAPTER 4:

A Categorisation of Fetters – External Fetters

In this chapter, we will look at the specific fetters that affect humans and cause suffering on all levels. The awareness of these fetters denies us happiness in life, so we will examine a comprehensive list of them. To make it easier, they are split into external and internal fetters. The main difference is that external fetters can be affected by external factors, while internal fetters are mainly determined by an individual's make-up (both physical and mental). Of course, there is not a clear-cut distinction between external and internal fetters, and both may affect us in multiple ways. For example, a bodily fetter will affect us internally, but it is primarily affected by factors external to our body.

Bodily fetters

Fetter of hunger

This is a fetter that everyone can understand and has experienced at some point in their life, probably often. Few things are as unendurable as an empty stomach for a prolonged period. Hunger is still one of the main fetters that millions of people in the third and developing world suffer from every day. Shamefully, it's also still a fetter for children in developed countries, who have to go to school with an empty stomach every day. Without this basic need being met and the fetter of hunger being removed, to even talk about happiness in life is laughable.

Fetter of thirst

Go out for a 10-kilometre walk without any water on a hot summer's day. You will certainly feel the effect of this fetter! You wouldn't get very far before you became exhausted and dehydrated. On such an occasion, the sensation of thirst would be far stronger and quicker than the need to quell hunger.

Fetter of coldness

Just as hunger will constantly remind you that your stomach is empty, the coldness sensed by your hands, feet, face, and entire skin when you're outdoors on a chilly winter day is a constant reminder to put more clothes on or find a warmer place. The cold and wet endured by someone on their first camping trip might be the fetters that dampen their enthusiasm for future camping adventures. Coldness is the fetter especially felt by the homeless in winter. There is no space for happiness in our mind when we're trembling constantly in a bone-chilling wind.

Fetter of violation of bodily safety

This fetter is the physical aspect of our bodily safety being violated. An example of this is if we were physically penalised by our parents as a child. The psychological aspect of fear related to physical violence can be classified as one of the mental fetters that often coexist with physical suffering. Physical abuse and its mental consequences are often the main cause of unhappiness for many children. Likewise, the torture happening in lawless or warring countries is truly a nightmare for people living in these places. The fetters caused by torture, injuries, and worse — the constant fear of such torture, injuries, and violence — is one of the reasons why people living in such countries can seldom feel happy.

Financial fetters

Mortgages, credit card debts, unpaid bills, and other debts and obligations become fetters to us once they pass a level we're comfortable with or go beyond our ability to handle them. The extent to which they negatively affect us depends on our relative tolerance towards them and how far we have slipped towards a point of no escape. This fetter affects a lot of people in today's society on varying levels — from a nuisance part of modern-day life to something so severe that it can cause some people to commit suicide, overwhelmed by financial disaster.

We live in a "credit era", a time of buying now and paying later, a time when pleasures occupy our mind far more than financial prudence. Unfortunately, as with most things in life, we have to pay back what we owe, and not just financially. There's the nervousness or fear every time the phone rings after a debt collector has called. There's the lingering frustration after a conversation with an aggressive debt collector, or the reluctance to open the mail after missing a few payments. There's the worry and fear of losing everything, of being unable to provide for your family's basic needs, or your house being repossessed by the bank if you lose your job. These concerns are felt by many people, particularly during an economic downturn. Moreover, these are the sufferings we must bear when in debt to someone else. Then there are the criminally high interest rates charged by credit card companies, which can devour the lion's share of our meagre after-tax income, making us truly their slaves for years to come.

This fetter may be the result of our attempts to avoid or postpone other fetters, such as failure to meet the basic needs of ourselves and our families, or due to a natural catastrophe, such as a fire burning down our insufficiently insured house.

Today, it's almost inevitable that we will assume some financial fetters. It's a necessity and a reality of modern life that nearly all of us need a mortgage to buy our homes or a credit agreement to buy a car. Owning a home in a modern-day, developed country is regarded as a symbol of achievement. However, to own a home, we must usually take on a mortgage that will be a burden for decades. For as long as we haven't finished paying off that mortgage, it will always be on our mind, because it's a large chunk of our monthly income gone.

A mortgage is a big financial burden for ordinary people, but it's not the only one. There are many other financial obligations that we cannot avoid in life. After buying our home, there are the costs of renovating and decorating it. There are further financial burdens when married couples start to have children. Raising children and providing enough money for their daily life and education is a big financial responsibility for many families.

However, the biggest reason why most people cannot enjoy financial freedom (satisfaction) until retirement[51] is the urge or desire to keep up with the Joneses, no matter how well off they are in material terms.

The need to keep up with, or be better than, the Joneses will always push us to the limits of our financial capacity. We want to look good in other people's eyes. These people include our co-workers, friends, neighbours, family members, and so on.

The desire to appear as winners and not losers is the most important thing in our lives, consciously or subconsciously. For some, everything they wear, from head to toe, has to be the latest fashion trends or the best colour, quality, and style. Boxes and boxes of shoes and stacks and stacks of clothes pile up in our wardrobes. The iPhones and gadgets we carry have to be the latest version, even if our old one was well above the basic requirements. Thousands of pounds are spent on new apparel for kids at the start of the year, even when their old clothes still fit perfectly and are rarely worn. This is the "rat race"[11] we try to win in life. We don't stop trying to be better than other people until we reach the limits of our financial capacity. It's the urge to win this "rat race" that has all people — not just low and middle-income earners but most rich people as well — trapped in the financial fetter for most of their adult lives.

Unfortunately, life isn't easy for ordinary people. Pleasures are the only things that most people know will provide relief, even if only temporarily. As a result, if they don't show enough prudence, some people fall into the trap of financial fetters in an effort to escape other fetters in life by pursuing pleasures.

Environmental fetters

Environmental fetters are easy to understand; they've become more of a problem to the modern man than to our ancestors. Pollutants in the air, water, and land not only pose serious threats to our health but also trigger our direct negative mental reactions. When someone from a developed country works or pays a visit to a third-world country, one of the hardest things to bear is the frequent, chaotic, deafening noise of the streets or the suffocating, inescapable exhaust fumes in the heart of a jammed city.

Noise is an environmental fetter that we have to bear daily in today's society due to the over-population of our towns and cities. The ubiquitous background noise of the city may not be an overwhelming problem to someone who has got used to it, but it becomes a challenge and even a luxury to find a quiet place for a moment of peace in our hectic city lives.

Fetter of disasters

Disasters are ruthless fetters capable of ruining our lives overnight. Without warning or reason, we may lose our property, loved ones, health, or even our lives in natural disasters such as earthquakes, hurricanes, mudslides, fires, etc. What's more, man-made disasters such as war, genocide, or persecution may have brought more pain, suffering, atrocity, and death to humanity than any natural disasters in recorded history.

When in the middle of a disaster, an individual's well-being and fate is entirely at the mercy of powers beyond their control. When disasters strike, they can be traumatising and have long-lasting effects on our lives. Some people never recover from these fetters, succumbing to them and becoming a victim of them.

Economic and financial crises are another type of disaster that can affect huge amounts of people. The Great Depression and the financial meltdown of 2008 onward were social disasters during which a whole generation was affected. The Covid-19 pandemic that started in January 2020 devasted the whole world in just a few short months. In the U.S. alone, it had infected about 4.4 million people and over 150,000 died from the disease by July 2020.[52] By June 2020, the unemployment rate was at a record high since the Great Depression.[53] This fetter will linger for many years for people in affected countries.

Disasters are capable of changing life courses for anyone and in any circumstance. However, it's only afterwards that we can truly recognise their impact on our lives and be humbled by the limits of our human capability to control such events.

Social fetters

Interaction and relationships with other people are a double-edged sword when it comes to our happiness and our lives. On one hand, humans are social beings, and it's a universal phenomenon that most of our happy time is spent with family, friends, and others at events such as family dinners and holiday gatherings. On the other hand, dysfunctional or acrimonious interpersonal relationships can make our lives unpleasant.

A mean boss, unfriendly co-workers, an abusive spouse, or a school bully can take a toll on our mental and physical health. So much of our energy can be consumed in negative environments that we often feel anxious and exhausted, making our days seem hard and long. When we're in such dysfunctional relationships or have such negative interactions, the future may seem hopeless. Depending on the setting and characteristics of such relationships, we can roughly divide social fetters into three sub-groups: political, intra-family, and inter-personal.

Political fetters

This fetter is easy to understand because it relates to freedom as we would normally understand it. The freedom to form and participate in a political congregation, freedom of speech, and freedom of religions are the cherished standards of a civilised democracy. It has even been said that you cannot truly appreciate political freedom until you've lived under a oppressive dictatorship.

Only very few — those who harbour political ambitions — might suffer directly from the political fetter. However, almost every citizen in a non-free country will suffer from the derivative fetters often associated with the political one. Social injustice, corruption, violation of private property, and other rights are all too often a heavy burden on an ordinary person's life in a corrupt, malfunctioning society.

Intra-family fetters

If you ask any couple, they will have a unique story to tell about their relationship with their other half. A stable, non-acrimonious relationship with a life partner is not only important but a *necessity* for a healthy and satisfactory married or co-habiting life. Unfortunately, a lot of people will probably tell you a story that's rough and tough instead of smooth and amicable. The high divorce rate in modern societies gives testimony to this.[36]

A physically or mentally abusive husband or wife can be traumatic for their partner and children. In many traditional societies, women have to deal with and suffer from the fetter of dysfunctional intra-family relationships due to the traditional values of marriage or for the well-being of their children.

Another important aspect of the intra-family fetter is living with family members who are suffering from mental illness. There is a huge and significant negative effect on happiness for those who marry or have a romantic relationship with someone who has a debilitating mental illness. [54] Likewise, for the family of someone with a mental illness, there will be an effect due to social or family fetters if they regularly have to deal with the person's mental illness and its effects.

Even in a "normal", non-abusive family situation, arguments or fights over matters from education to who should wash the dishes occur more often than most people would like to admit. These seemingly small but omnipresent problems can turn life into an endless marathon. When a family faces a period of stress and uncertainty, such as moving to a new city, changing or losing jobs, or suffering from a severe disease or mental illness, this fetter can be aggravated and make life miserable.

The importance of these relationships to us and the long periods we spend with family members means that intra-family relationships hugely affect our sense of happiness and well-being. The negative effects of a broken family can affect its members not only at the time but for a long time afterwards. It's very difficult for a child to eliminate these negative impacts completely, even well into adulthood.

Other inter-personal fetters

It seems to be part of our nature that our behaviours and sense of wellness can be affected greatly by others around us. It doesn't matter whether you are a teenager, a mature and strong adult, or in your senior years — people around you will always affect you in some way.

How we think, what we do, and how we feel is significantly affected by our peers, the customs and traditions we grew up with, and the society we live in. Peer pressure can be the dominant fetter that affects our sense of well-being, especially during adolescence when we're starting to be aware of — and care very much about — our image in the eyes of others. At this stage of our lives, when we're still mentally immature and more sensitive to peer pressure, bullying can be a significant cause of distress. The devastating effects of bullying on school children are well-documented.[46] It can also create negative effects that last far beyond our school years.

To a certain degree, Freudian psychology concerns the extensive effect on an individual's mental life of the intra-family and social fetters experienced in infancy. This fetter not only causes teenagers to have low self-esteem and develop all kinds of unhealthy mental and behavioural patterns, both at the time and long after, but it can even lead to suicide.

Everyone suffers from social fetters, but their type and magnitude can vary greatly between different cultures and countries. The more rigid and strict the moral standards and custom requirements, the more severe the fetters are to people in that society. Traditionally, in Oriental countries such as Japan, people worry more about social fetters than those in Western countries do.[55] These fetters are at their least significant in some Latin American countries and countries like Bhutan where people take life less seriously, and places where the culture is more lenient and tolerant.

In the next chapter, we will look at internal fetters.

CHAPTER 5:

A Categorisation of Fetters – Internal Fetters

In this chapter, we will consider the internal fetters that affect our happiness, that is, the fetters inherent to us and affected by internal factors. Importantly, it's arguable that these internal fetters play a more influential and significant role in our happiness than the external ones covered in the previous chapter.

Fetters of ailments and illnesses

This category of fetters includes all types of illnesses, diseases, and conditions that cause pain. This is one of the main causes of suffering in human beings. Almost all of us suffer from these types of fetters daily as an adult, particularly in our senior years. This is perhaps one of the main reasons why kids seem to enjoy life so much and have more fun than adults; they normally have less of these kinds of fetters.

When it comes to our conscious mind, any pain caused by illnesses or non-ideal conditions will dispel the fleeting moment of happiness we just sensed. These types of fetters can befall anyone, rich or poor, noble or common, anywhere in the world. When the fate of illness befalls someone, they will seldom taste the sweetness of a happy life, particularly when the illness is severe or there are many.

Often, it's not the life-threatening dangers of illnesses that cause suffering, but the constant pain and discomfort caused by some seemingly "minor" conditions that make life unbearable. The recurring headache caused by a migraine, the plugged nose caused by hay fever, the energy-depleting, body-and-soul tiredness of chronic insomnia, and the hopeless day-and-night cycle of depression are examples of the truly miserable parts of human life.

When we're in the middle of such conditions, nothing seems capable of helping us; treats or words from others don't seem to matter to us anymore. Even love from others who truly care about us and who we cherish cannot prevent us from falling victim to suffering. The only drive left in our mind at such moments is to escape the unbearable pain and endless, uncontrollable, depressive thoughts. When strong enough, these fetters can strip us of everything that makes us who we are. Some even long for the wings of death to come in the night, stealing them away, so they don't have to bear another day of living hell.

Mental fetters

More than anything else, our mental condition affects how we feel about ourselves and how happy we feel about our lives. Mental fetters, whether in the form of negative emotions or chaotic thoughts, can wreak havoc on our lives. But also, the majority of external fetters can only affect us *through* them. Typical negative emotions include but aren't limited to hatred, guilt, anger, resentment, hostility, scorn, grouchiness, phobias, worries, distress, drowsiness, grief, sadness, sorrow, fear, jealousy, shock, astonishment, nervousness, and so on.

Unlike external fetters or physical ailments, which we get the occasional break from, mental fetters are omnipresent. They reside in every corner of the world and at every level of society. Rich or poor, civilised or barbaric, king or slave, saint or common, none save an exceptional few are exempt from them.

All normal humans are slaves to these fetters (by "normal" I mean the vast majority of humanity; what constitutes an "abnormal" human being will be explained in chapter 10). Throughout recorded history and even the oral history of ancient time, the majority of literature and art has been the record and testimony of humanity's struggles with these fetters. Almost every soul on this planet is tortured by mental fetters for practically the whole of their life. Even the optimistic "positive psychology,"[33] has to admit that 50% or more of our feeling towards our lives is determined by the "set range" of our internal traits.[56,57]

All classical religions are largely teachings, wisdom, and techniques to help humanity liberate itself from the mighty demons that have haunted humans for millennia. Most people abandon their battles with these demons and surrender. We use the term "human nature" to describe their power over our lives and deem them an inevitable part of being human. Some cultures and religions use other terms such as "sins", "sufferings", or "bad karma" but equally deem them to be an unavoidable, unchangeable part of human life.

The main realm of psychology, psychiatry, and derivative techniques such as psychoanalysis and cognitive therapy are basically the study of these fetters and how they can be dealt with. Most mental illnesses, disorders, or abnormalities (particularly non-organic ones) are extreme examples of the suffering these fetters can cause. Schizophrenia, depression, melancholy, neuroses, and post-traumatic stress disorder (PTSD) are some examples of this.

The scope of the problems created by mental fetters is so vast, it's no exaggeration to say that most psychiatric research (and therefore the bulk of a trainee psychiatrist's curriculum) is about the manifestations and results of these fetters, and the means of dealing with them. The harm that these fetters can cause is not limited to mental illnesses or mental disorders. Many other pathological symptoms are also related to them directly and indirectly. Insomnia, stomach ulcers, and neurodermatitis are just a few examples.

It would be impossible (and is also not this book's intention) to list and describe every mental fetter and every effect they can have on our lives. The few discussed here are just some of the most common and easily understood.

Fetter of negative emotions

Hatred, anger, rage, and resentment can be classified as one big group of mental fetters that affect our lives, not only individually but also collectively, with tremendous implications. No other emotion does more harm to us physically or mentally. An old adage says, when you're angry, you get a taste of hell. Anger consumes our vital life energy, leaving us feeling exasperated. We may feel a desire for revenge or cruelty after we perceive we've been badly or unfairly treated, stirring up similar reactions to when we feel hatred or resentment. Such feelings can consume our time and energy for years after the event. Hatred and revenge can breed vicious cycles that destroy the lives of individuals, families, or whole countries. These destructive cycles can last for generations, as witnessed throughout history and in some parts of the world today.

Terror, fear, worries, despair, nervousness, and sadness belong to another category of mental fetters that deeply affect our lives. They have the potential to be even more troublesome to us than anger because they're more stable and longer-lasting, as shown by depression. When you're severely depressed, you have no interest in life and feel down and dark all of the time. Day and night, you drown in a sea of endless despair without sight of any hope. Severe chronic depression can be regarded as one of the worst conditions to have and the extreme wrong end of the happiness scale.

Guilt, shame, jealousy, and scorn are other negative emotions and thoughts that stop us feeling good about ourselves, our family, or our society. They happen to almost everyone in every society much of the time. However, the degree that a person is affected by these emotions depends on their culture and family background, as well as their individual make-up.

There are many more negative emotions than those I've mentioned, and their number and severity will vary from individual to individual. However, they all have two things in common: firstly, they appear to be more "internal", and secondly, they cause bad feelings, pain, or suffering to us. When we're in the grip of any of them, we cannot feel happiness.

It's safe to say that almost everyone is familiar with the majority of the negative emotions listed here on a daily — if not hourly — basis or even worse. The difference between individuals is the degree to which these negative emotions occur and how long they last. When we're prone to such negative emotions, we're usually labelled as "pessimistic" or "worrisome" or told that we have a "hot temper".

Fetter of mental noises

Loneliness, boredom, and background mental noises are some descriptions of our regular state of mind. They constitute the fetter that has probably been the least-studied but that affects almost every one of us. The regular state of an ordinary mind is not still or blank when there's no external stimulus. As Csikszentmihalyi[13] puts it, psychic entropy or psychic chaos are normal states of mind for ordinary people when not engaged with other people or focused on any particular activity. Together with another fetter of low overall stamina, it forms the general basis of mental and sensory life for the vast majority of adults. [13]

All kinds of thoughts and ideas are constantly coming and going in our minds. Bizarre things appear in our minds at the least expected time, and we are often puzzled why we have certain thoughts at certain moments. We appear to have no say in what comes to our mind or when, like a passive receptor receiving whatever is being broadcast. For example, it seems strange that right at the moment of success, instead of enjoying it, we hear a clear voice of disapproval in our head. Lying on a tropical beach, with a picture-perfect azure sky and turquoise water, we should be mentally and physically relaxed, but instead, we're busy worrying about issues in the mundane life that we longed to escape in the first place.

This fetter is not some small nuisance in our life; it has mighty, omnipresent power over how we feel about life, and it can even determine our future to some extent. Freud and Jung tried to explain its origin in the misplacement of the "libido" or the manifestation of an individual or collective unconsciousness — "archetypes". [58]

This fetter has haunted human beings since the dawn of history. We have lived every day of our lives under the influence of this fetter without knowing it, due to us accepting it as the normal way of life. Only when it becomes out of control do we and professionals recognise its existence and effects. It's well-understood and well-documented that some mental illnesses and conditions are caused by stimuli or thoughts that our consciousness loses control of and is overtaken by, as is the case with schizophrenia[45] and partially with Attention Deficit Hyperactivity Disorder (ADHD). The "voices" we hear in our heads, the relentless ranting, and the weird imaginings are all too common among us. Ordinary people may not know their nature but will know their effects only too well!

Stop reading for a moment and pay attention to the thoughts and ideas in your mind.

What have you found? Thoughts and ideas come and go in a flash and you seem to have no say over them at all. A vivid description from a schizophrenia sufferer, as quoted by Csikszentmihalyi, provides us with a clear picture of how these fetters affect people in daily life: "Things just happen to me now, and I have no control over them. I do not seem to have the same say in things anymore. At times I cannot even control what I think about." … "Things are coming in too fast. I lost my grip of it and get lost. I am attending to everything at once and as a result, I do not attend to anything."[13] Of course, one does not have to suffer from schizophrenia to experience this.

When we feel bored, we're also clearly under the influence of this fetter. We feel bored not because our mind is clear or tranquil, but because we're tired of the mental noises that occur when no external stimuli are strong enough to dispel or smother them. We're bored and restless when the whirl of thoughts and weird ideas becomes too much for us to handle, so we try to run and hide from them. This is why we turn our music up so loud and have to immediately turn on the radio or music as soon as we get in the car. It's because the stuff in our head is worse and more difficult to bear than stuff on the radio. We just cannot bear this fetter when there's nothing external to mask it. The whirlwind of thoughts in our mind — whether trivial, bizarre, or meaningful — consumes our physical and mental energy.

Together with the negative emotions that often accompany them, random and uncontrollable thoughts can be tiresome and draining, depleting our vital energy at every moment. We feel tired all day, from the moment we open our eyes in the morning to when we go to sleep at night. This is where the "Sunday morning blues" comes from and is one of the reasons why we feel so tired when we should feel relaxed at home on a Sunday with nothing to do. [13] It's also one of the reasons we're preyed upon by the entertainment industry. Movies, games, and all types of speculative sports are nothing but relief from our endless internal ranting and erratic emotions. The reason why we need to be "entertained" is to escape from these fetters, even if only momentarily. When we're freed from these tyrants for an extended period, we feel like we've found true happiness, which is praised as "optimal experience" in *Flow*.[13]

Another clear display of this fetter is insomnia. Insomnia, or difficulty falling asleep, is a problem that arises when we cannot stop thinking when we need to. Anybody who's had trouble sleeping may remember that the more they try to sleep, the harder it is to stop thinking and let the brain rest. No matter what we do or how we prepare for sleep, these thoughts keep showing up, which is tiring in itself. The more we worry about (not) falling asleep, the more frenetic our thoughts become.

The folk wisdom of counting sheep to block annoying thoughts sometimes works and gives our brain precious time away from this fetter to let us recharge. But when the fetter is strong and persistent, as in the case of chronic insomnia, we can suffer from extreme physical and mental fatigue. Our mind is distracted and we find it hard to focus. Severe chronic insomnia is one of the worst conditions that a human being can suffer from. In some cases, it can lead to suicide.

The fetter of chaotic thoughts is the background mental noise of our everyday life; the background against which we play out the episodes of our own drama. When we're freed from the external anxiety of our hectic, professional jobs and sit down beside the fireplace in our cosy home, when we seek solitude in our favourite corner of the garden after a hard day at work, or when we gaze at the horizon on holiday in our favourite place, we still have these uncontrollable thoughts to deal with. They are unwelcome guests but they come anyway. When we're tired of the negativity of others, we have the option to walk away, but we're stuck with the never-ending chatter of our brain for a lifetime.

Our enjoyment of anything is, to a large extent, determined by how strong this fetter is. The quieter or weaker it is, the happier we will be. When it's loud and strong, our worldview darkens. In such a state, we're bound to get easily agitated by people or things happening around us, even very early in life, and we have difficulty maintaining healthy and stable relationships with others.

When our mind is melancholy, it can affect us for the whole of our lives. It dooms us because no matter how lucky we are in life regarding wealth or fame, how successful we are in our business or profession, we just cannot drive that sad feeling away for more than a few moments. It dooms us because contrary to popular belief, our ability to learn and be educated is determined more by the magnitude of this fetter than by how smart we are or how hard we work.

As clearly recognised in the case of ADHD, there is simply too much noise going on in our children's minds, making it extremely difficult (if not impossible) for them to focus on learning for a reasonable length of time. Difficulty focusing is not just limited to the young or those with ADHD though; it affects learners of all ages and can affect every one of us in our daily life, particularly in our jobs.

Mental fetters are part of our character and personality or are manifestations of more fundamental elements inside us (these will be discussed in more detail in book two). They're a part of our being as ordinary humans, the same as our hands and feet are. The only difference between them and our hands and feet is that we can't see them. Negative emotions and chaotic thoughts occur more through reaction than intention. In other words, we do not *will* them; they're reactions to internal or external stimuli. As in physics or chemistry, an action causes a reaction. Negative emotions and chaotic thoughts are natural reactions to the stimuli we receive in a given moment. The only control we have over such thoughts is how and if we want to express them.

Emotional Intelligence (EQ) describes our ability to handle these emotions and thoughts.[59] However, the reaction occurs whether we express it or not. The culture, customs, or manners we learn from childhood onwards tell us how to deal with the negative emotions and chaotic thoughts that come to us, as well as the proper way to express or suppress them, but they cannot stop the thoughts from occurring. Nobody wants to be angry, scared, guilty, or sad, but these feelings come to us when circumstances arise. We may wish we could be calm, confident, grateful, and happy all of the time, not just in a few exceptional circumstances, but our emotions and our minds have a will of their own that is often stronger than our own will. More often than not, our rational thinking will fall victim to our emotions.

With regard to how happy we feel about ourselves, the role of mental fetters cannot be over-emphasised. They account for the vast majority of how we feel about ourselves, our families, our communities, and the world. The strength of our negative emotions, and how we deal with them, forms the basis of our EQ, which may have more influence on us than our IQ.

David Lykken points out that we have a unique set point — our own range on the happiness scale.[56] It's my opinion that this range is mainly determined by our mental fetters. It has been said that the pre-depository set point accounts for about half of our perceptions of how happy we are.[56,57]

Mental fetters are the main factors that separate individuals living in the same society with similar environmental factors (income, living conditions, etc.). They are the main factor in distinguishing our individuality, making us who we are. They are the main cause of suffering in our daily lives, and they are also the main source of conflict in our relationships with others.

Sages are all similar, but each ordinary person has their own problems. In short, mental fetters are the root of most of our problems. Money or other material possessions cannot save us from slavery to these menacing mental fetters, something that even the wealthiest of people come to realise. For example, the great comic genius and Academy Award winning actor Robin Williams committed suicide at the age of 63 due to severe chronic depression and other health issues. He had already accomplished everything that a man could have accomplished; became as successful, rich, and famous as a man could be; and his career seemed to be thriving. Yet despite all that, he still committed suicide. You see, you could live in a multi-million-dollar mansion and own the most luxurious bed, but that wouldn't help you have a good night's sleep if you had chronic insomnia. In despair, a lot people resort to alcohol, drugs, excessive sex, binge eating, or partying for temporary relief from such fetters. But every party has to end and the euphoria induced by substances will wane. One has to face this reality when the party finishes and the reality of the fetters returns.

This is to say nothing of the other negative by-products of temporary reliefs such as health problems, which will add to one's future fetters. Money can buy you a party; money can buy you alcohol, drugs, or even sex. However, money can't drive these mental fetters away after the party, after the sex, or after the euphoria of drugs. Afterwards, we still have to deal with the vast majority of our daily lives, which inevitably is under the control of our mental fetters.

It was once said that poverty is the root of all evil. Another saying suggests that greed is the root of all evil. I believe that mental fetters are the root of all evil. The vast majority of substance abuse, prostitution, domestic violence, broken families, racism, and crimes are directly caused by mental fetters or desperate attempts to fend off the unbearable pain they cause. This can culminate in physical self-abuse: people pull out their hair, mutilate their bodies, and lacerate their faces in an attempt to divert their minds from unbearable, unstoppable feelings or thoughts.[46]

In today's Western countries, with the advance of material wealth at all levels of society, mental fetters affect our lives more than ever. The fetters of basic needs such as food and clothes are no longer a pressing concern for most. Medical, scientific, and technological advances have improved the hygiene standards of our daily living, significantly reducing our physical ailments over the past few centuries. Yet there has been little progress made in alleviating the mental side of fetters for millennia. Instead, we're under attack from external stimuli more than ever before. People have become far more self-centred, seeking greater sensations in life without concern for morals. Individualism is now the default mainstream mindset of our hedonic age, and as a result, mental fetters have become more prominent than ever before.

Fetters of desire

Desires, oh, these desires! These mighty desires not only drive the majority of lives but have occupied the minds of many great thinkers throughout history when it comes to happiness. Desires can be defined as things we need or want but don't yet have.[16] In that sense, they're something we lack. And like most things in life, desires have a negative side.

Individually or collectively, desires are at the centre of all human life. To the average person, the purpose or goal of their everyday toil is merely to satisfy their desires. Desires have become more than just life goals; they're now life itself. From the basic instinct of a baby sucking milk from its mother's breast to the accomplishment of all we want to achieve in our careers, desires encompass most, if not all, human activities. These desires are what we need and want every day of our lives. It's no exaggeration to say that all industry, trade, commerce, and most other key activities in our society are created and driven by the desires of people.

To most intellectuals, the Enlightenment — the dawn of the modern era — was to a large extent the liberation of human desires, particularly bodily ones, from outdated superstitions or religious dogma. The countless philosophical treatises about human goals and human happiness since Ancient Greece have, almost without exception, centred around the desires of humans and their satisfaction. Our desires seem an inseparable part of us and we cannot imagine life without them. We may even feel that without desire, we are somehow endangered.

One of the biggest blunders that humanity has ever made is mistaking happiness as being the satisfaction of desires rather than freedom from fetters. Sages of all cultures have tried to teach us similar lessons, only for us to dismiss their words as wishful thinking and empty idealism. We opt instead to waste our time and energy in endlessly pursuing the satisfaction of our desires. Throughout history, desires have been everlasting invisible chains — pulling, pushing, and dragging humanity through the everyday struggles of life.

The lure of desire has trapped us yet we remain largely unaware of the negative effect it has on our lives. For most of us, the satisfaction of desires is the highlight of our day. The rich, fragrant latte after work, the fun and excitement of watching our team win, the first bite of our favourite dish, the time-stopping absorption of playing our favourite games, and the heavenly exhilaration of orgasm are all things we look forward to during an otherwise stressful or boring day. To the vast majority of ordinary people, these are regarded as pleasures, fun, and enjoyment. They're the goals, the reason we work hard and endure difficult lives.

It's not easy to comprehend desires in the same black-and-white way as other fetters. The satisfaction of our desires, or even the hope of satisfying them, gives us such a pleasurable feeling that we regard them as the purpose of life, not as liabilities. Some of our desires, such as the desire to do well for ourselves and others — and overcoming difficult circumstances to do so — are truly noble aspects of humanity. However, a desire becomes a fetter to us if we suffer when it's not satisfied. There is nothing wrong with having some desires in life. The question is what they are and how strongly we feel them. When they become too many or we feel them too strongly, they inevitably cause frustration, dissatisfaction, and discontent.

With desire comes an uncomfortable feeling of wanting something we don't have. Hunger is the feeling of an empty stomach, making us desire food. Thirst gives us the desire to drink water. Both hunger and thirst are uncomfortable feelings, fetters we try to avoid. Most desires have similar negative sides and so become fetters in need of satisfaction. When desires are strong and plentiful but their satisfaction is limited, the "hunger" or "thirst" to satisfy them can become all-consuming, blocking the path to happiness.

Desires are unlimited; our time and resources are not. We regularly have to choose between competing desires. In today's fast-paced society, there are often multiple demands on our work and personal life. Without a healthy balance, a happy life will be difficult to achieve, even if we achieve success in one area. For example, we might highly value career success, but this is often achieved at the expense of spending quality time with our family.

Another consequence of the quest to satisfy our desires is the negative side effects it can have on our health and finances. These negative side effects, or fetters, can be both short and long term. Even a seemingly simple pleasure, such as a meal at our favourite restaurant, entails the short-term downside of feeling bloated and sluggish afterwards. Not only that, but the long-term consequences of uncontrolled food consumption — obesity, increased risk of cardiovascular disease, cancer, and even premature death — are some of the many future fetters that we risk suffering for a moment of pleasure.

Extreme fetters of desire: addictions

When desires become extreme, we become slaves to them, as in the case of addiction. Desire as a fetter cannot be demonstrated more clearly than through addiction. The pleasure or release of tension when such a desire is satisfied — and the pain when it can't be — makes it much easier to understand desires as fetters. Nobody can deny an addict's pleasure when they get their fix or their suffering when they go "cold turkey".

The desires of ordinary people during everyday life are similar. The only difference is the degree of pleasure and suffering involved. The insatiable appetite for junk food in America has turned obesity and being overweight into a national health crisis.[60] The pleasure felt in wolfing down a double cheeseburger or the frustration when your favourite item isn't on the menu that day is comparable to the desires and sufferings of a drug addict. Who could argue otherwise? The craving is so strong that we throw all of the warnings and advice about junk food's effect on our health out of the window. The vast majority of regular human desires have similar characteristics and so can be called mild or medium addictions. If we believe drug addiction and alcohol abuse to be problematic and not a source of happiness, then we can easily understand normal desires as fetters.

Non-materialistic desires

Materialistic desires are not the only desires that hamper our lives though. Some non-materialistic ones can have a far more significant negative effect on our lives without us even being aware of it. Expectations, preferences, and assumptions all form parts of our desires. They're the wishes, wants, and "should-be"s of our everyday life. We want our partners to remember important dates, such as our birthday or anniversary, and for them to give us a romantic gift on those days.

We want our children to be "perfect", work hard, get excellent exam results, and be highly regarded. We want our contributions at work to be recognised by our boss or our co-workers, no matter how insignificant. We impose our views and judgments, which we assume to be right, without remembering that they're simply our opinions, our preferences, choices, or desires.

When our expectations aren't met in life, when reality conflicts with what we want to happen, we become disappointed, frustrated, or even angry. We're unhappy with our partner for forgetting the anniversary of our first date. We're frustrated with our children for getting a C amid a run of straight As. We're jealous of our co-workers when our boss praises them but doesn't mention us. We blame others, the company, the weather, dishonest politicians, and so on for our negative emotions or our bad mood. We complain about everything in life, from trivialities such as a table not being laid properly to world affairs. We complain about the people around us when they don't meet our expectations. So many of us are just angry at the world without knowing why!

We don't realise that the cause of most, if not all, of our disappointments in life are our desires. The real world can never match the ideal we have in our heads. Frustration in life is inevitable, a certainty if we're overly occupied with our expectations and desires. No one, not even our spouse or our children, can ever live up to our idealised expectations. We can't even match our expectations of ourselves, which is the reason for so many of our negative feelings of regret and guilt! How can we then expect others to match our ideals?

Many couples argue and fight over trivialities, ruining otherwise good marriages without realising that most of their differences are based merely on preferences. The stronger a person's desire, the greater their disappointment and unhappiness when it's not achieved. That's why a perfectionist is seldom happy and an easy-going person is often more content.

Desires that are not fetters

However, it must be noted that not all human desires are fetters. The desire to end the injustice of apartheid in South Africa, even when incarcerated, did not bring pain to Nelson Mandela. Instead, it inspired him to endure the hardship of imprisonment. The desire to help the least fortunate in our society, even if circumstances mean we can't help as much as we'd like to, doesn't cause us misery but uplifts us — even if our altruistic desires aren't fully satisfied. We might get a noble or spiritual feeling from helping others or the environment, even if we're contributing to an end goal that won't be reached anytime soon.

Such desires are inspirations rather than fetters. When performing good deeds or even contemplating them, we feel an energy within us, perhaps even a connection to something bigger and more powerful than us. It may not be immediately apparent, but we feel an inner joy, peace, maybe even bliss seldom felt during everyday life. It's a higher state than when our basic, routine desires are filled. At such moments, we feel the purpose and meaning of our life; the meaning not only of our efforts but our failures and sufferings too. The gut feeling that we're doing the morally right thing makes our suffering bearable. A lack of it, even when our regular pleasures are being fulfilled, can leave us feeling "short".

Those more mundane desires, whose unsatisfaction doesn't cause us suffering, are not fetters either. Having no food is a fetter to a hungry person, but it's not to someone with a full stomach. A professional athlete will be upset if they are offered a contract below what they expect, even if that contract is worth millions of pounds. The average person won't be affected by this, save perhaps a faint notion that they don't have, nor are likely to ever have, millions of pounds. They're more likely to be upset when a colleague gets a promotion or a pay rise and they don't. The strong desire for recognition in their job becomes that person's true fetter.

The self and the ego

Desires and mental fetters are a big part of our inner self. We identify the "self" or "ego" as residing in our brain and heart. The frightening self resides inside us, beneath the deceitful and frivolous exterior of civilised etiquette. They're the internal factors that dominate our life. As Robin Williams once lamented, "I am not really this happy; we all have our own deals; you have got yours and I got mine. If we laugh in the interim, that is great, because we've still got our deals to deal with, so why not a little laughter?"[61] Desires, mental fetters, and chaotic minds are our life's own real "deals".

Exterior conditions, wealth, fame, or power mean little and are little help against them. Even love from our life companion, family, or friends — the most precious gift that a human could receive — may only help a little in the struggle with our internal demons. It can't save us from the relentless, hopeless sadness of severe depression and other bad deals. This is why sages tell us to "look within" and "seek freedom within", not reach for outside glories such as wealth, fame, or power in the search for ever-elusive happiness.

Mental fetters, monkey mind, and burning desires are the monsters inside all of us that we must struggle with every day, from minute to minute. They are the mighty demons haunting us from when we're so young that we're barely aware we exist … until we die. They are the dark side of a human.

Mental fetters are the forces that shape not only the route of our life but its fate and destiny too. They are the karma of our lives that we want to break free from but eventually succumb to. They are the root cause of us constantly making the same mistakes in life. The situations may change, as may the players, but as humans — we play the same game with the same heart-breaking results over and over again. As Willa Cather said, "There are only two or three human stories, and they go on repeating themselves as fiercely as if they had never happened before." [62]

Faced with so much pain, trouble, and suffering, ordinary human lives are truly depressing without the relief of positive experiences. Pleasures provide that relief that sustains us in our long struggle with life.

CHAPTER 6:

The Positive Side of Experiences

An ordinary human being's life is a dynamic equilibrium between positive experiences, such as pleasures, and suffering, which results from fetters. Even though for most of us, our lives are not as bad as having all of the fetters listed in the previous chapters, or having them all at the same time, fetters engulf our hearts and minds for so much of our waking day that there is little time for anything else. The net weight of most people's fetters is so heavy that they barely experience anything else, except when their heart and mind is occupied by positive emotions or experiences.

It seems that we lost the innocence of our pure mind (or as close as we ever got to it) after our "babyhood" years. This was a time before we had any sense of our self, and it varies from person to person. Some babies' innocence seems to last only a few months before they begin showing awareness of their individuality through aggressive behaviour. Others may keep this innate innocence until the age of 6 or 7 years old, when the "I" or "my" awareness finally befalls them. After that innocent stage, we're on the standard journey of life: a process with forces of positive emotions and experiences on one side and fetters on the other, forming a dynamic equilibrium. Due to the kaleidoscopic human characteristics and circumstances that each individual has to face in life, no two lives are identical. Although the dark side of this equilibrium — the fetters — fundamentally determine how happy our life is, it's the other side — the positive emotions and experiences — that give life its rich tastes and colours.

Episodes of positive emotions and attention-demanding processes within an otherwise uninterrupted current of fetters are the nature of the human life process. Pleasures, positive relationships, engagement, and pursuing goals or ambitions (whether meaningful or not) are the pleasant side of the dynamic equilibrium of life. This is the side that is always the focal point for ordinary people.

However, we don't clearly or fully understand the true nature and limit of the role played by the positive side of experiences in our lives. As with pleasure, positive feelings such as pleasant emotions and experiences only temporarily shield us from our fetters. When we're engaged in something, particularly something interesting or pleasing, we forget about our fetters and our suffering. These are the moments when we feel happy. The engagement (or resonation) that brings us this precious moment of happiness can be an engagement with somebody, as in a positive relationship, or engagement in an activity, such as playing a game.

Positive relationships: engagement with other people

Positive relationships bring pleasure and relaxation, either by themselves or in combination with other things such as good food, drinks, etc. Quite often, they're the most basic, important ingredients of happiness in the lives of ordinary people. Humans are social beings and our best time is often spent with other people. Sometimes, we can't describe the warm feeling we get when a loved one is close by or the pleasant atmosphere at a reunion.

This is why we overcome many obstacles and travel long distances just to attend annual family gatherings. Parents and grandparents are so happy when their children and grandchildren gather around them at times such as Christmas. Food, drink, and presents do bring pleasure and happiness to the occasion, but they're secondary. The mere presence of children and grandchildren can often be the highlight of the whole year.

A simple family reunion brings joy to a family, even if their financial conditions cannot support the luxury of a banquet or expensive gifts. Food and drink at family gatherings are far more enjoyable than the same food and drink consumed alone. The joy and happiness we, and more importantly our loved ones, experience is the reason why the biggest annual migration — over 100 million people — happens at Chinese New Year.

It has been proven by researchers that married men and women are much happier than those who live alone or are divorced.[8;9] A loving, caring, positive parent, grandparent, sister, or brother will bring us the happiness of being a family member. With shared blood and many fond memories, positive resonance with people at traditional gatherings gives us precious moments of worry-and-care-free relaxation that we seldom experience at other times.

Positive relationships are not limited to family though. They exist whenever we interact with others and can affect our happiness in all kinds of situations at every stage of our lives. The thought of being isolated and outcast is often one of our biggest fears and the source of our most painful memories. On the other hand, positive engagement with people and the feeling that we are appreciated, valued, and cared about by others is the thing we cherish most in our work or private lives.

What a wonderful life it would be if only positive sentiments, emotions, and feeling existed in our families, schools, and working environments! As we know, however, such perfection exists only in our dreams, wishes, and maybe in another world. The reality of life is that there are negatives attached to almost any relationship. After marriage, we find shortcomings in our partner that seemed non-existent before. Altercations, big or small, happen far more often than during the honeymoon period.

Parents are so difficult to please that no matter how hard we work and how well we fare, it's never enough for them. Misunderstandings, belittlement, betrayal, physical and emotional abuse, or feeling unappreciated can cause pain and suffering to us at the time. They may also stamp deep markings on our memory that can profoundly affect our feelings about ourselves and our interactions with others. These negative feelings and emotions are social fetters in our lives. When they're strong and many, life can become hard and strenuous.

In most cases, life is a love/hate situation where those we love the most are also those who hurt us the most. The family who give us so much support, security, and laughter are the same family who make us feel not good enough, betrayed, angered, saddened, or abandoned. It's the way of life that the positive side of a relationship necessarily entails a negative. When the negative side becomes overpowering, we're forced to abandon that relationship, whether by moving out, getting divorced, or quitting our job — either way ending up in solitude.

Loneliness: Lack of engagement with people

When we've been emotionally hurt by someone, we might cry out "leave me alone!" Of course, being left alone is only preferable in comparison to the pain we're experiencing at that moment. As almost everyone knows, being alone or in solitude is no paradise for the hurt and bruised. Loneliness does not feel good at all. As quoted here originally from Aristotle "Whosoever is delighted in solitude is either a wild beast or a god." [63] For the vast majority of us, being alone leaves us at the mercy of our inner fetters of negative emotions and chaotic thoughts. Lonely people are often in a highlighted state of anxiety and alertness to a perceived hostile environment.[64]

Being alone is not the preferred choice, but it's a choice that people end up with when relationships become too difficult or painful to deal with. For many mentally ill people, living alone is, sadly, almost the natural result for them. It's often very difficult for people with severe mental illnesses to maintain stable long-term relationships with others.

Nobody wants to be lonely; young homeless people don't live on the street because they like the hardship or loneliness of street life, but often because of an abusive home too harsh and toxic to endure. Perhaps their mental conditions are so chaotic and violent that their family couldn't cope. For kids who are mentally ill, living on the streets may be the result of them or their families exhausting all attempts at living at home within bearable limits.

The same goes for suicide; people don't kill themselves because they like death but because it's too hard for them to live! Likewise, people don't live alone because they like to be alone, don't enjoy love, or don't enjoy being loved, but often because it's too hard to handle the inevitable negative side of a relationship — when there are too many negative emotions and bad feelings in the relationship. When being in a relationship with others is too much, people are forced to accept the choice of being alone.

Engagement in activities

The second type of situation in life that allows us to escape from fetters is engagement in activities. Engagement in activities is more essential to human life than relationships with others; imagine life without activities! A person may even choose to live without engaging with others — a hermit, for instance. But no one, other than those in a persistent vegetative state, could live without engaging in some forms of activity. Even the slowest of creatures, the sloth, has to fill basic biological needs to maintain its life.

We engage in all kinds of activities at every stage of our lives, and with these activities, we fill every page of our life journey, bringing colour and content to our life. Without them, this book would be blank. In fact, the variety of activities that humans can engage in are limitless. Some are important in bringing us happiness, so it's worth us getting a clear understanding of them.

Flow

Flow is a term first coined by Csikszentmihalyi[13] to describe the mental condition when a person performing an activity is fully immersed in feelings of total focus, full involvement, and enjoyment in the process. The key to Flow is becoming absorbed in the subject we're engaging with or the activity we're doing. In my opinion, all of the other aspects of Flow described by Csikszentmihalyi are not necessary, such as the complexity or challenging aspect of the task we're doing.[13]

Case Study: Soccer Flow

I like to play basketball and golf. I enjoy skiing, swimming, and snowboarding, but football (soccer) is the only sport I love and enjoy so much that it gives me a distinct Flow experience. When I play football, I forget about myself entirely; I'm totally absorbed in the game. My self-ness, the separated "I" is gone. "I" is integrated seamlessly with the game that I wish could last forever. Hours have gone by even though I feel that the game kicked off just a few minutes ago. Even the danger of injury when playing on a rough, hard, sand-and-clay pitch can't dampen my enthusiasm. Bruises cover my legs, knees, and feet. Sometimes, new injuries occur before old ones have healed. But such physical pain seems a small price to pay for the fun and excitement of running, passing, and kicking that ball! Winning or losing, playing with friends or strangers, none of it matters. If I'm playing football, I leave the outside world on the side lines and dissolve myself in the rhythm of dancing with that magic ball. That Flow experience remained unparalleled until I was 35 when I experienced other abnormal happiness. It's no overstatement by Csikszentmihalyi to praise Flow as the "optimal experience" for ordinary people.[13]

As research has shown, other factors mentioned in Csikszentmihalyi's theory beyond absorption (such as challenge, skill, a clear goal, feedback, and growth of complexity) are often by-products of a process but aren't the must-have ingredients for Flow to happen.[65] When a person is in the midst of experiencing Flow, what they're doing is so interesting that they forget about themselves, their surroundings, and whatever else is going on in their life. They are totally absorbed and their mind is 100% occupied by the task at hand.

The tasks that fascinate people in this way can be amazingly diverse: sports, dancing, music, collecting the weirdest things imaginable, you name it. The only common trait is that when people experiencing Flow are deeply absorbed by what they are doing, everything else is almost irrelevant. The reason for this irrelevance is that only the deep absorption of our attention on the activities we're doing can mask all of our fetters from our consciousness.

An activity such as pulling the lever of a slot machine all day might be dull to most people, but it may be the most attractive thing imaginable to a gambling addict. The absorption experience in Flow is always created by a "voluntary" intention of a person who loves the thing they're doing and has fun doing it. It's not forced upon the person by somebody else, nor is it forced by a biological impulse from the self, as in the fun-less behaviours of compulsive disorder. When an activity is not wholly voluntary or for the sake of the activity itself, it's most likely a sub-Flow experience (which will be explained in more detail later) or one of the stresses that are fetters to us.

The Flow experience is created over a long period during which our consciousness is totally and thoroughly free from all of the fetters that we would otherwise be gripped by. The experience of Flow itself must also be a positive one — fun and pleasurable. This is what separates Flow from other deeply focused experiences, such as "fight or flight". In fight or flight, people are also completely focused and absorbed by a situation, because it could be a matter of life or death, so everything else is suspended. But nobody enjoys or likes fight or flight situations because they're a fetter. They're actually the person's biggest fetter at the moment they are experiencing it.

As Csikszentmihalyi[13] pointed out when he coined the term "Flow", the name may be new but Flow has probably been experienced by people since the dawn of humanity. Before modern times, people derived Flow experience from the arts, and it was a universal phenomenon in the East and the West. In the long history of China, the harp, chess, calligraphy, and painting were regarded as symbols of a good life, the activities enjoyed by the upper class and nobles. In Western traditions, arts such as music, painting, and literature were regarded as the route (other than in religious experiences) to relief or even a "salvation" for human beings. The salvation was not religious but from "the terrible driving force of the will" to quote Schopenhauer. "The storm of passions, the pressure of desire and fear, and all the miseries of willing are then…calmed and appeased in a marvellous way. For an instant, we lose ourselves as we step into another world."[16]

Flow, in its pure and ideal state, is not a common experience. Many people may never experience it in their lives except during childhood, a time when they fail to have full and clear self-awareness of it. A Flow experience is not a natural "human right" that everyone could or perhaps should have. Instead, it seems more like a privilege reserved for those blessed with luck in life — not counting the gambling addicts whose addiction is more a curse than a blessing. It certainly seems that Flow is beyond reach through willpower alone. The majority of us have to make do with sub-Flow, which is far more common among the vast majority of ordinary people.

Sub-Flow

Sub-Flow is a term I coined to describe a human life experience in which we focus on doing things with a clear goal in our mind but where our absorption is not as complete as it is in Flow. Although we are more focused than when we have nothing to do or when we have no clear goal in mind, we cannot block all of the worries, pain, and random thoughts from our mind. Quite often, the things we're focusing on doing are difficult and require our effort to accomplish, rather than being effortless as in Flow.

In sub-Flow, the goal is the most important thing, whereas, in Flow, the process is. Quite often, the goal is all that drives someone to undertake sub-Flow activities. Winning for the sake of winning and making money for the sake of making money both belong to sub-Flow. The goals in sub-Flow experiences are desires in our lives, so sub-Flow constitutes the vast majority of our life activities and occupies the major part of our life. When we establish a goal, we organise our activities to fulfil that goal, providing a framework for a normal life episode. The parts of the process that fulfil the goal have meaning only within the context of that goal. Thus, the goal creates meaning for human activity[13] and is the key to providing a structure that organises both our consciousness and any activities subsequently executed towards that goal.

Formal school learning is a largely sub-Flow process and experience. It's not like volunteered learning, which is willed by the learner and could be described as a Flow experience. For kids who love playing video games, learning a new game is usually a Flow experience even if they are frustrated during the process. However, school learning is an obligation, a task assigned by other authorities. As a kid, you most likely go to school not because you want to, but because you have to. It's a fact of life that all kids go to school; there seems to be no other option (home-schooling does provide another choice but is a rare exception).

Our learning in school is almost always passive and we have no say in what we learn or when we learn it. When we go to school, we have to follow the rules set by teachers and are constantly reminded of the consequences if we disobey them. Although a subject may be interesting and can attract our attention when we're lucky enough to have a good and enthusiastic teacher, school learning itself can seldom attract our attention enough to cause a Flow experience. Even for the smartest students in a class, learning subjects in a formal curriculum, such as maths and languages, takes a lot of effort and energy — a far cry from the effortless effort of Flow. We may have one subject that interests us, but it's near-impossible for anyone to have a deep interest in most of the subjects we have to learn at school.

With the pressure and stress of competition in our grades and performance among classmates, school learning becomes even more burdensome and is disliked by most students. It has even been referred to as a prison for kids.[66] As children, we cannot help but wish that class would be over sooner and feel that summer break is our saviour from long, demanding classes and hard homework.

Another important sub-Flow experience is work. The vast majority of jobs are not Flow but sub-Flow experiences. A few extremely lucky people find a dream job that matches their interests. Apart from them and the lucky few who manage to make a career from their hobby such as professional musicians, most of us experience sub-Flow in our jobs.

First of all, jobs are necessities; we need a job to support ourselves and our family. Most of us have to take whatever job we can find and most of the time, we have little to no say in what that job entails. Our jobs are based on what we have to do, not on what we want to do, but on what our bosses and circumstances dictate.

Jobs are jobs! Obligations and tasks we're paid to perform. We're required to perform to certain standards and within specified restrictions such as deadlines and budgets. These externally-sanctioned standards and restrictions cause us worry and anxiety. They are fetters to us, destroying the worry-free, care-free atmosphere of a Flow experience even if we truly enjoy our work.

This understanding can explain the "paradox of work", a phenomenon observed by Csikszentmihalyi in his research using the "experience sampling method".[13] People at work feel skilful and challenged, meaning they feel comparatively better, stronger, more creative, and more satisfied than during their leisure time, when there's generally not much to do and their skills are not being used. During leisure time, therefore, people tend to feel more sad, weak, dull, and dissatisfied. However, people generally want to work less and have more leisure time!

At work, we do have the benefit of focusing on the job at hand, meaning we don't have the opportunity to pay too much attention to other, less-urgent, matters and even some of our mental fetters. To focus on one's job requires a lot of energy, especially in overcoming common difficulties such as picky clients, demanding bosses, workplace politics, relationships, job security, and the challenges of the work itself. It's a far cry from the effortless effort found in a Flow experience. Particularly in today's fast paced-workplace, the demands of a job can be overwhelming, making it a stressful, demeaning experience, and becoming a fetter rather than a pleasure.

True flow vs. sub-Flow

A true Flow experience is a specific process unique to each individual. Even the majority of recreational activities we undertake for fun fall way short of being Flow experiences, belonging instead to the category of sub-Flow or at best a combination of Flow and sub-Flow experiences.

Case study: the Flow of football

Since childhood, I've been an outdoors enthusiast, taking part in all kinds of outdoor activities and sports including playing with mud, hide-and-seek, water buffalo-riding, hiking, ping-pong, badminton, basketball, volleyball, running, soccer, swimming, canoeing, kayaking, skiing, snowboarding, and golf. Of all the sports I've tried, only football has ever given me that distinctive quality of absolute absorption (as you saw in the previous case study). It has nothing to do with my talent or skill level — I'm as bad at football as any other sport because of my below-average co-ordination skills. It also has nothing to do with the challenge level, as skiing, snowboarding, and golf are certainly more challenging to me than football in skill requirements, while kayaking, swimming, and running are less challenging. But only football has that connection for me. I like to ski, snowboard, or golf, particularly with my family or friends. However, when participating in these sports, I'm always "fighting the mountains" or "fighting the club". Moments of "floating on snow" when snowboarding or exhilaration when hitting a perfect golf shot are few and far between. Most of the time I spend playing other sports involves me learning to play rather than totally immersing myself. Going on a family skiing weekend is more to fulfil my obligation as a father than for the pure enjoyment of skiing. I'm still separated from skiing even when speeding down the slope. I feel the pain when the speed puts too much pressure on my leg bones. On the contrary, when I collide with an opponent playing football, I often don't mind or even notice the collision. I'll regularly ignore the pain — if I feel it at all. Golfing for me is more of a social outing where enjoyment is found in the company of good friends rather than the golf itself. Only football has that magic touch that transforms me.

As mentioned, winning for the sake of winning is a sub-Flow experience. Although we enter into games as a player or spectator voluntarily, we don't enjoy the process as much as in Flow but are driven instead by the urge to win. Winning is the only goal of playing a game and the sole purpose of watching one. There is no regard for the game itself, which is certainly enjoyable if — as in Flow — its beauty and speed become the centre of our attention.

When playing a game for the sake of its process, with pleasure or fun found in either winning or losing, it can even become a Flow process. However, in a sub-Flow process, where a game is played purely for the sake of winning, people become angry and upset when they're losing. This is the character of the sub-Flow experience of winning for the sake of winning only. As winning as the only concern, dirty play and all kinds of cheating in sports or competitions are characteristics of sub-Flow.

However, there is rarely a clear-cut distinction between Flow and sub-Flow activities. It's more often a mix whereby we have some fun and take interest in a process, but the chief aim is the final result. To a degree, we enjoy the process of performing a task, such as our work, but the pay we get for it is just as important to us, if not more.

Most of the activities in our daily lives are a shade of grey mixed from the black and white of Flow and sub-Flow experiences. We go to work for the pay we bring home, but we enjoy the work experience as well, particularly when we work with nice, caring people who we have mainly positive interactions with. On the other hand, we engage in most of our recreational activities for fun, although fulfilling the obligation of a family role, such as a parent, is also clearly on our mind, such as when we play the same game with our children over and over again or watch their favourite film for the hundredth time.

However, most of the time that we're engaged in these "mixed" activities, we don't reap the benefits of total absorption found in Flow. Instead, we experience our "normal" mental state, with all of its inherent emotions and thoughts. How much we enjoy the activity — and the level we achieve on the "Flow" scale — is affected by how deeply we're engaged in the activity and how strong the background noise is from our brain. When we have the energy and we're not so burdened with worry, even the silly games we play with our kids can give us true fun and enjoyment.

Although sub-Flow is not as ideal as Flow in terms of the feeling or sensation that the process gives us, it nevertheless plays a very important role in human life. As we saw earlier, the end goal is the key part of the sub-Flow process, initiating it and driving it forward. The goals in our lives are our desires, ambitions, and aspirations, therefore Sub-Flow experiences encompass the vast majority of human life processes.

Almost all important human life processes, such as school learning, jobs, political ambitions, and business enterprises are sub-Flow experiences. As we discussed when looking at school learning and work, we don't enjoy the activities of sub-Flow processes as much as we do Flow processes. Nevertheless, they provide two crucial ingredients for human life.

First and foremost, they give our lives meaning and value, even if we dread them. Most kids would rather not go to school, and they may even hate going, but they understand learning — and learning well is vital for their future. With that in mind, they accept schoolwork as being of value for their future careers. We may hate our jobs, and we may hate the boring work routine that makes us feel more like a machine than a human being, but we accept it because it's the only way we can put food on the table and keep a roof over our heads.

However, a more important role that sub-Flow processes play in our life, unrealised by most people, is the provision of a long-lasting task that focuses our attention and drives away most of the fetters from our consciousness. Such tasks constitute the vast majority of human activities on earth, the duties found at the different life stages for each individual. Like them or not, we bite our lip and get down to them; the father or mother who provides the family with bread and butter, or the factory foreman who faithfully performs the same routine for years.

We walk our life's journey of ups and downs with the fulfilment of these duties being the main task of our existence. Only on occasional pauses do we find our breaks: a drink at our favourite bar or watching our team play at the weekend. We never give enough credit to the duties in our lives that require us to get up at 6am and drive our kids to school or go to work from 9 to 5. We treat them as dreaded obligations instead of something we like to do. We never realise their vital function of giving us important relief from troubles or conflicts at home or relentless attacks from our mental fetters. Only when we lose these obligations — when we're jobless, for instance — is their true value revealed to us.

Why is it called sub-Flow?

Bearing in mind the importance of sub-Flow tasks in masking our many fetters, you might wonder why it's called "*sub*-Flow". The "sub" prefix relates only to the level of happiness felt during an activity; it has nothing to do with their moral sense of importance in our lives.

On the scale of happiness, Flow experiences are the best human life experiences, the icing on the cake. Only a lucky few get the chance to enjoy them. Pleasures are cakes without icing, available to the majority of ordinary people. They may not be the best, but they're still cakes and they still give us some delight in life. Sub-Flow experiences are bread and butter. They don't taste as good as cake, with or without the cream, but they prevent us from going hungry. Many people will never experience Flow in their lives, but some pleasures make life bearable and meaningful, even for those who seldom experience pleasure, such as the extremely poor.

However, when we lose our goal, lose something to strive for, we find ourselves in the worst human scenario imaginable. That's the plight that haunts some of those living on aboriginal reserves in Australia or North America, or inner-city neighbourhoods in major metropolises. Desires, ambitions, and aspirations provide direction, structure, and organisation in our lives. Without them, we would fall victim to the chaos of an aimless, meaningless life.

The balance of positive and negative experiences

Most of the time, positive life experiences are not one thing: pure relationship, pure engagement, pure goal pursuit, or pure pleasure, but are organic combinations of two or more positive processes. We often engage in Flow activities with our close friends: we go on holiday or do something pleasurable with family members. We participate in meaningful volunteer work with people of a similar mindset and sense of comradeship.

We often engage in activities far less interesting than Flow with people who we have both positive and negative feelings about, as is normal in a common workplace. We're pushed and pulled in life by events that give us different, mixed feelings. Extremely strong emotions, positive or negative, are relatively few during a typical day. Most of the time, we're under the prevalent mental state that is our mood, the background noise of our mental fetters, including the non-stop chatter of chaotic thoughts and simmering emotions.

The minds or conscience of ordinary people, their awareness at a specific moment in life, is a constant struggle between positive experiences, such as pleasure, and the negative experience of fetters. It's the battle of a lifetime. Every moment in every day of our lives, we're either feeling pleasure or suffering from fetters. There's seldom a moment in life where one is truly free from either.

There is no true, long-lasting tranquillity or stillness for ordinary minds during which no fetter is attached or no pleasurable activity is required to expel fetters from our minds. Only on rare occasions — when we're free from both external stimuli and internal mental fetters — may we glance that fleeting moment of conscious stillness.

Strong emotions, whether positive ones such as exhilaration or negative ones such as rage, aren't frequently felt in everyday life. Instead, it's our mood that occupies the vast majority of our waking hours. The conditions and tone of our mood are largely determined by the mental fetters triggered by the events of the day, whether at home or at work.

Understanding human life experiences

The dynamic nature of human life experiences cannot be emphasised enough in establishing a clear understanding of life in the real world. Neglecting either the positive or negative side will lead to a misunderstanding of how lives are lived. Emphasising the importance of fetters is not as pessimistic as people may think; it simply reveals the full picture of life as we experience it. Without realising the dynamic nature of positive engagements and fetters, life will remain a confusing paradox to us. Why is money so important when it can't guarantee happiness? Why are the richest countries in the world not the happiest? Only when we consider both sides of the dynamic equation is it possible for us to understand the true nature of our lives.

One consequence of this equation is that the equilibrium may be altered to increase happiness in two ways: a small negative side (fewer, weaker fetters) or a large positive side (more, stronger engagements or pleasure) will both result in a happier state. This is why for an innocent, worry-free 5-year-old, almost any activity in life can bring pleasure and fun, no matter how trivial. However, to a mentally ill individual, the mental fetters are so strong and so many that almost nothing can dispel the terrible inner feelings and chaotic thoughts, rendering them incapable of pleasure — **anhedonia**. The majority of us are neither as lucky as that 5-year-old nor as unfortunate as a severely mentally ill person. We have our own share of problems, worries, troubles, and challenges though. We might feel basic fetters of deprivation such as hunger and cold, and we'll probably have financial fetters such as debt, and no doubt have our inevitable share of social fetters no matter which family or country we're born into.

Social fetters are the main external fetters that significantly affect our happiness. If we're born into a country under a dictatorship or a corrupt or dysfunctional government, we'll experience the pain of life under the rule of tyranny, injustice, or chaos. Even for those living in a free and democratic society, social fetters such as discrimination, physical or mental abuse, bullying, and broken families are all too common.

Social fetters are also the main factor in separating countries from each other in the overall happiness of their citizens, with relative material well-being measured by indices such as gross domestic product (GDP). Denmark and other Scandinavian countries have topped the list in recent surveys on world happiness. [11,67,68] They are the countries with the best social safety net and social environment.

Citizens of these countries have universal healthcare, which has the benefit of both taking care of them when they're sick and giving them peace of mind (rather than worries of how to pay hospital bills). Compared with US, these countries are also safer and have less crimes.[69] Parents in these countries don't need to worry so much about the safety of their kids at school because of tighter gun laws than in, say, America. There is far less social discords among citizens, so a sense of true engagement and belonging to the community is possible.[68] Compared with third world countries or emerging market countries, these countries are all free countries with relatively well-developed democratic governments, so the evils of corruptions are less burdensome. [68]

Law, order, and trust within a society are intangible but extremely valuable to the vast majority of its members with regard to their happiness. When you have to worry about the safety of the food you eat or the water you drink, when you have to be alert about who you can trust on a daily basis, life will be hard, troublesome, and tiresome. It's a big burden on every citizen in countries where businesses put profit before the health and safety of consumers, particularly when such an issue is severe and widespread. It's the same with other public goods and services.

When trust within a society is low, there's no sense of community among its members, and life becomes full of potential dangers, worries, and uncertainty. All of these things become fetters. This is perhaps one of the main reasons why China, Russia, Eastern European countries, and former-Soviet Union republics have lower happiness scores in recent surveys than other countries with similar income levels.[10,67]

Despite this, the most dominant fetters in our lives are internal. The fetters of our physical health problems, mental fetters, and desires are the decisive factors in our happiness equation. When we have serious problems with our physical or mental health, happiness is elusive, if not impossible. Conversely, when we have a healthy body, fewer or weaker mental fetters, and fewer insatiable desires, small things in life can bring us fun and pleasure, and we are contented with what life has to offer.

A healthy homemade meal, a bouquet of flowers, or the glimpse of a white cloud on a sunny, blue-sky day can bring us delight when our hearts and minds are not too heavily burdened. This means that you don't need to envy Academy Award parties and the like — as such things are nothing but ego battles. There's no true fun for many of the celebrities attending such events if they are struggling with worries about their appearance and whether they'll get enough attention. Instead, the best fun to be found may be at a house party with simple dishes, a beer in your hand, and your friends. In this place, your body and mind may both relax — as long as you don't have any severe internal fetters in the first place. Replace this with whatever experience works for you.

The journey of life

Living a human life is like sailing non-stop on an endless, stormy ocean for a lifetime. Pleasures and positive experiences are lonely islands dotted in the ocean's middle, and only when our boat passes by them do we experience calm water. The water of that stormy ocean is the fetters in our life. Most of the islands are tiny. They are regular pleasures and are many, but so small they can barely offer a moment of relief. Some rarer big islands shelter the forever-moving boat of life from the relentless and ruthless elements for a precious, longer time. These are positive engagements with people, such as a loving partner, or healthy hobbies that provide optimised human experience and existence such as Flow.

But for the vast majority of our lives, we're out on the treacherous water. The journey on that endless ocean, the journey of our life, is overwhelmingly determined by the conditions of the ocean, the turbulence of the sea, and the gusts of wind. How do we feel about life? How happy do we feel from moment to moment? How happy do we feel overall? The answers to all of these questions will be determined and characterised by the strength and number of fetters in our life.

At the outset of our journey, as we leave the harbour, the water is calm and the elements friendly: the innocent time of childhood. Most of us enjoy our childhood even without many material possessions. The day goes by easily, and fun seems effortless. Some playmates are the only thing needed for a joyful hour or a whole weekend of enjoyment. However, there are still risks of early-life fetters, such as being born into an extremely poor family in a wealthy society or born with rare and severe physical or mental health condition such as leukaemia or autism. The biggest and the most common fetter for a child, however, is being born into an abusive or broken family, without much love or care. These children learn very early that life isn't easy and can be incredibly painful.

During adolescence, we become more conscious of ourselves and how others see us. Peer pressure starts to become our fetter. We still have a lot of fun but we start to experience more negative emotions and excessive desires too. We want more and to be better than our peers. If we live in a society that demands academic achievement and rankings, as most Oriental countries do, then we'll feel and have to bear the burden of competing with others from a young age.

With more demands from parents and society and more desires than circumstances allow us to satisfy, we become more rebellious, oscillating between joy and hopelessness. It seems that right at the end of our teenage years, our mental apparatus grows to full, adult capacity. With this new mental capability, we have to face a whole spectra of mental fetters, which won't make life any easier than before. To make things more difficult for us, this happens between the ages of 20 and 30, when we have to face all kinds of challenges: establishing a career and perhaps a family.

The demands from our families, our careers, and ourselves are at their peak. We have so many ambitions, desires, and wishes that there's rarely a moment when we don't feel the stress, pressure, anxiety, or restlessness within and between.

With uncertainty and inexperience in our careers and relationships, we often have to deal with the worst of life's emotional struggles. With the establishment of young families comes the tasks and obligations of bearing and raising kids. All of the demands, desires, and difficulties we face during this period of our life contribute to the phenomena that around this age, we experience one of the lowest periods of our life on the happiness scale.[70]

With the passing of each year after early adulthood, we gradually establish ourselves in our careers. Our tasks and obligations at home become lighter as our kids grow up to become teenagers and enter college or university. More importantly, we get used to the key relationships in our life. Divorces have terminated really bad relationships and we've developed the best strategies for maintaining healthy relationships, so we may experience less turbulence than before.

We have also become veterans in our profession, meaning there is less of the uncertainty that caused so much anxiety and stress at the beginning of our careers. No matter how we fare in our jobs or business, we have most likely come to terms with ourselves and are less burdened by too much ambition or unrealistic expectations.

For most people, the years before retirement are probably the best years of adulthood. Their kids have grown up and left and the mortgage has been paid off. Most of the desires that drove us crazy at a younger age lose their lustre, and we're more content with our lot in life. A stable and mutually understanding companion, a hobby, or some close friends in a social circle are all we need to be content in life.

Those golden years would be picture-perfect if it weren't for the gradual onset of health problems. After approximately the age of 40, we start to notice more obvious problems with our body. We gain weight much faster than in our younger years, and these extra pounds show in our bulging bellies or bottoms. With them come the worries of high blood pressure, high blood sugar, and high cholesterol. We have more aches and are sore all over our bodies, reminding us of the fact of ageing more than anything else.

Health issues are the dominant concern and main fetters in our senior years. Sickness, and the fear of getting sick, not only causes pain and suffering directly, but can also result in financial difficulties if we're without a well-covered health insurance policy in a country that requires one. In fact, one of the leading causes of senior bankruptcy in the U.S. is excess medical expenses.[71]

After long and relatively calm senior years comes the inevitable end of life, the end of our journey, death. Many people not only don't understand death but are scared to death of death. Unfortunately, it's reasonable and understandable for people to be afraid of death because it seems to not only devour everything we have and value in our lives, but because experiencing it is so painful.

Most lives don't end in a calm and pleasant way, but in a stormy and painful one. Severe and terminal illnesses such as late-stage cancer not only bring unbearable pain, but can also deprive us of the privacy and dignity we cherish so much in life. We come into this life crying and leave it crying in pain, save for the few lucky ones and very few abnormal people who leave on their own terms. When life ends in a calm, painless, and speedy way, it is truly a blessing for human beings.

In summary

Even though it is the negative side of life (fetters) that have the decisive influence on human happiness, it is the positive side of human experiences that give life goals, meanings, and colours. There are two main kinds of positive human experiences: positive relationships with other people and activities. Positive relationships are one of the most important ingredients of everyday happiness for ordinary people. A lack of these is the main reason why people feel lonely or isolated. The activities we do every day seem essential to a human life, as they bring us fun and relief from fetters.

Flow is acclaimed as the optimal life experience.[13] When people do Flow activities, they enjoy the process so much that they don't care so much about winning or losing as they lose themselves in the activity. Although Flow is the best possible experience for ordinary people, it is not the most important experience for ordinary people. Many people may never experience Flow in their adult life. Instead, ordinary people's main activities are sub-Flow. In sub-Flow, the goal is the only concern (motivation) for people doing the sub-Flow activity. The goal in sub-Flow is our desires in life, and sub-Flow activities encompass the vast majority of human activities. School learning and jobs are two examples of typical sub-Flow activities in most people's lives.

CHAPTER 7:

Delusions and Mid-Life Crises

Through determination and hard work, things like wealth, power, and fame are achievable to man. With luck, health and beauty are also possible. But happiness — true, long-lasting happiness — is out of reach for humanity, at least for the vast majority of ordinary people. In this chapter, we'll look at the various delusions that affect humans, and mid-life crises, which is closely related to them.

Delusion of money

At the beginning of our lives, we learned that candy is sweet and that the coins our parents gave us could buy that candy. The candy tasted good, gave us pleasure, and made us happy. Later on, we found that many other things gave us a similar sensation to eating candy; we identified them as "the goodies". We also found that playing games gave us a sense of gratification, particularly when we were winning the game. The trophy we got for winning identified and reinforced that personal experience. The game is life and the trophy is money, cold cash, the thing that can buy all the other things we want in life that make us happy. We don't need anybody to tell us that the candy is sweet and that we like the sweetness. It seems obvious; nobody needs to question the fact that candy is sweet, just as nobody needs to question whether day is bright and night is dark.

We identify fun, laughing, and pleasure with the goodies, such as food, wine, the latest technology, fresh flowers, or the newest fashion. We also find fun and pleasure in occasions such as parties, carnivals, and holidays. We watch all kinds of TV for entertainment and watch celebrities living lavish lives of money and fame. We are forever bombarded with omnipresent commercials trying to convince us that only *their* product will make us happy. Our personal, intimate experiences of gratification when receiving a gift such as a favourite toy or having a drink at our favourite bar after a long day convince us more than anything else that money *can* buy us happiness.

In this hedonistic age of wealth and fame worship, it's a given that for most people, the accumulation of money is in our best interest. Naturally, to live a happy life, one must make more money and beat the competition. All other considerations, such as religious teachings and ethics, are for the benefit of others or for the public at large. The unequivocal goal for an individual is to make and keep as much money as possible. A happy life will naturally follow.

Why can't money buy happiness?

It's been observed since time immemorial that money alone cannot buy happiness[5], even though common sense dictates the importance of money in our lives. Research shows that money does have a positive correlation with our happiness, at least at an individual level.[72] It's almost a given in this age of hedonism that money will always serve the best interests of the person who has it. However, people are often astonished that they don't find the paradise they expected when great fortune befalls them, such as a lottery win.

For many, it's a rude awakening, particularly for those regarded as rich and successful, that money alone doesn't buy them lasting happiness. Even if we end up with more money than we could ever have dreamed of, more than our peers and more than enough to keep us comfortable for the foreseeable future, we still don't find ourselves in the dreamland we expected. Instead, we find that we still suffer the same overwhelming troubles and worries as before. Or at the moment we accomplish something we've been working so hard for — a project, qualification, or sporting medal — we suddenly find an empty feeling inside after only a moment's jubilation. Quite often, it's an awkward emptiness that doesn't make sense to us because it comes when we finally reach the goal we've worked towards so long for and put so much effort into. It's a weird, uncomfortable feeling between the completion of one goal and the setting of another. Without a goal as the focal point in our life, everything seems to lose its meaning, and we lose direction.

How many of us have bought into the dream lifestyle of the rich and famous as portrayed on television? A luxury yacht, endless wine, and a pretty or handsome partner is a typical "rich and famous" scenario. For ordinary people, it's difficult (if not impossible) to understand why those lucky few — the rich and famous, the film stars, pop stars, and sporting heroes — still have trouble in their lives, so much trouble that they come to rely on alcohol and other addictive substances for relief. It's even more difficult to accept that some of them choose to commit suicide.

It's clear from the happiness theory proposed in this book why money is important and helpful in life for happiness: it easily eliminates the fetters of essential basic needs such as food, clothes, and shelter. Enough money can relieve us of financial fetters (and the mental fetters they can trigger). Money can satisfy many desires, particularly materialistic and egotistical ones.

Unfortunately though, the fetters that chain us in this life aren't limited to just these few. We have fetters related to our health, both physical and mental. We have fetters in our emotions and our chaotic mind activities, which are totally outside money's control. We have social fetters from the macro or micro environments we live in.

Money can buy us insurance for the best medical coverage, but it cannot buy us health. Money cannot guarantee us protection from cancers, strokes, diabetes, etc. It can't even prevent the common cold! Money cannot buy us a good night's sleep, no matter how luxurious and expensive the bed we sleep on. Money can do nothing to help us deal with conflicts we have with family, friends, or work colleagues. Money cannot buy us peace of mind, even momentarily, no matter who we are. Even the desires we thought could satisfy us — if we only had the money to afford them — offer no answers once we've fulfilled them. The satisfaction of old desires only makes way for new, more expensive, ones. As Schopenhauer accurately stated, "Yet for one wish that is fulfilled there remain at least ten that are denied. Further, desiring lasts a long time, demands and requests go on to infinity."[16]

The true essence of happiness is freedom from fetters, and money is capable of freeing us from some basic and financial fetters. It can buy some pleasures or moments of happiness, but never enough for long-lasting happiness, the ultimate prize.

The golden world associated with the rich and famous, which drives so many of the so-called "super-rich", is nothing but a bloated balloon inflated by ego, a delusion that leads many to their fateful end without realising why. Once the idea of making money becomes the main goal in life, many rich, artistic careers become deserts devoid of surprise, wonder, and enjoyment — leaving only the tangled thorns of competition and survival. What's more, a money-orientated, self-centred mindset often strains or ruins marriages and other important relationships.

Hedonism (in its entirety) and utilitarianism (to a lesser degree) both result from the delusion of money. The delusion of money is two-fold. The first is the view that pleasure comes only from money, the things we enjoy that money brings to us, or more broadly, the positive sensation we experience in life regardless of any other attributes or conditions of ourselves. We perceive that we have experienced both happy and sad moments during a normal day. The happy moments, such as time spent in a bar, are the times when we enjoy what money brings us and sad moments are the times when the outside world puts us down.

The perception of human felicity as "continual progress of the desire from one object to another, the attaining of the former being still but the way to the latter" has been the dominant view of pleasure since antiquity.[5] As we discussed, pleasure itself is only doing the trick of masking fetters from our conscious mind. No matter how much we enjoy the gourmet food we're eating or how fantastic our orgasm, they're but fleeting moments in the long 24 hours of a day. The rest of the time, we're at the mercy of our fetters. The strength and frequency of the fetters, and how many fetters we have, dictate how we experience our individual life.

As we've seen, money is limited in its capacity to reduce or remove fetters from our lives. When our mental fetters are so strong that they cause mental illness, money barely buys a moment of pleasure, as mentally ill people often suffer from anhedonia, meaning that nothing in life can bring them pleasure.

The delusion of money contributes to the popularity of lotteries. Lottery players are overwhelmingly blue-collar workers or poor people with little chance of becoming rich through their jobs or professions. They fantasise about buying their dream house, dream car, and dream holiday to realise their dream of happiness — if they could only win the jackpot.

The majority are aware that buying lottery tickets is a money-loser because the odds of winning are so small that they lose with every lottery ticket they buy. But the hope of winning the jackpot and their dreams of the lifestyle bought with vast amounts of money impels them to keep playing. Unfortunately, they could better use money spent on the lottery to ensure that they or their children don't have an empty stomach.

The harsh reality is that winning the lottery wouldn't solve the majority of problems for the people who buy lottery tickets. Buying that dream house, dream car, or dream holiday won't change a person's life for long, save for temporary gratification. The few prudent ones wise enough to use their sudden fortune to pay off debts or save towards their children's education are the only ones who truly benefit from winning in the long term, as they eliminate fetters from their life.

What's more, money can even bring us more fetters than happiness. As some lottery winners have found, winning the jackpot alienates old friends through jealousy. It can strain family relationships if the sharing of winnings isn't handled sensitively. With easy money to hand, people may choose to gorge on gourmet foods or engage in substance abuse, creating health problems.[73] All of these things explain why a recent study reported no long-term significant effect of winning the lottery on a person's happiness or mental health.[74]

The second delusion of money is the view that more money exponentially improves our life. It's this aspect that drives most of the world's already successful people.

White-collar crimes, those committed for money or other personal interests by people who are "doing well" in society, result mainly from the delusion of money. Ivan Boesky, the so-called "King of Arbitrage" in the 1980s, was a typical victim of the delusion of money. Before Boesky began insider trading by illegally obtaining inside information, he was already an outstanding success story in America.[75]

Through clever dealing and a "scientific investment method" claimed to be as precise as NASA's, he achieved massive success and respect in corporate America. He owned a 12-bedroom Georgian mansion set on 190 acres in Westchester County outside New York City and had a personal fortune believed to be worth between $100 and $200 million. He seemed to be a celebrity with limitless potential.

But somehow, Boesky resorted to insider trading, which he clearly understood was illegal, to make more money than he could have made "honestly" or legally. Illegally making more money for himself made absolutely no sense at that time, other than moving up a handful of places in the *Forbes* rich list, which from his wife's recollection seemed to be his motivation.[75]

Boesky had a lot to lose if he was caught, although he calculated that the chance was probably small. He risked his reputation, credit, business, fortune, and even his marriage and family — all of which he eventually lost. Even if he hadn't been caught insider trading, he still had to pay the price of worrying that he would be. He also lost the inner peace he enjoyed when doing honest business, as he claimed in his books and public interviews.[75]

Thus, if Boesky was aware that his illegal trading was for no other reason than improving his *Forbes* standing a little, and that it would entail all of these fetters, he surely only continued out of pure stupidity. Boesky was a shrewd businessman led astray by the delusion of more money. He genuinely believed that making more money, whatever the cost, would improve his life. As he claimed on his T-shirt, "he who owns the most when he dies wins."[75] This delusion reinforced his burning desire for more money, which triumphed over any rational thinking for his well-being. The greed to make more money at whatever cost seemed like an occult power that drove him to his fateful end.

The financial crimes committed by rich and powerful are almost always led by the same delusion that led Ivan Boesky to his fall. Unlike a hungry homeless man stealing a loaf of bread, who receives the benefits of pain and hunger relief, white-collar criminals don't provide themselves with many benefits. Grand-scale corruption committed by high-level government officials, which undermines the health and stability of many countries and societies, results largely from the delusion of money.

All over the world, since time began, those in power have always been the upper class, "well-to-do" members of society. Almost without exception, they are the well-fed and first-fed, even during times of war or famine. They are well above the level where more money can make any meaningful difference to their well-being in life. They're already well-paid and well cared for by society, and more money (even earned through honest and legitimate methods) will make almost no difference to their quality of life. For them, the fetters that money can remove no longer exist. The fetters that chain them in life cannot be removed — or even reduced — by more money. On the other hand, committing corruption will certainly undermine their well-being in life.

Corruption is illegal and condemned (at least in theory) by both authorities and society at large, no matter whether it's committed in a free or a repressive country. Even in a society with a culture, tradition, or tolerance of corruption, it's not an honour — not something you could boast of or tell your grandchildren. It's always something "under the table", something you have to hide from others, even when they're doing it too. Corruption is perhaps the number one way that a person falls from power, and the most efficient and deadly weapon that their political opponents have. People will generally not sympathise with the offender and will find it hard to forgive them, whatever the merits of their career.

The consequences of committing corruption can be severe, such as political and public ruin, and even jail. In some less tolerant countries, grand-scale corruption can lead to capital punishment, and for those involved in never-ending legal battles, the money they were so desperate to gain is spent on lawyers.

For those who have committed corruption but not yet been caught, fear and worry over getting caught will haunt them. For those who attempt to escape punishment, their life bears little resemblance to the life that someone with their wealth *could* be living. Such fugitives must hide all of the time to avoid being spotted, arrested, or deported. The anxiety and fear of living as a fugitive will haunt them before they are eventually caught, or for the rest of their life if they are not.

The delusion of success

"There is nothing more confining than the prison we don't know we are in."

– William Shakespeare

The delusion of success has been one of most confining prisons for humanity over the course of human history, more so than the delusion of money! Many people are aware of the delusion of money, realise the limits of money, and know that it cannot solve all of their problems. Few, however, realise the delusion of success.

Put simply, success is the holy grail of humanity. Many people don't believe in (a) God. Some don't believe in the power of money and despise pleasures. However, everyone in this world believes in success and wants it. A Google search for the word "success" brings up over a billion pages of related items, but it's difficult to find any that talk negatively about success. In fact, if you look at all of the *Happiness 101* style self-help books available today, you'll be surprised to see that what most of the authors are actually talking about is success and how to achieve it. In most people's minds, happiness and success are synonymous.

From the time we enter school, we're taught and encouraged to have the ambition to become "somebody" and accomplish "something". We're taught by our parents and teachers that we have to work hard to reach these goals and be successful. We're constantly asked, "What do you want to be when you grow up?", "What are your ambitions?", and "What are your goals for your future?" These questions are asked by almost every adult, teacher, parent, relative, or friend you meet. The examples set by our parents or mentors gave us the idea that life will be good when we become successful. This becomes a given that we never doubt.

Most of us will come to attribute our lack of happiness to either circumstances or our failure to work hard enough, saying "I didn't study hard enough, so my grades not only disappointed my parents but me too" or "I wasn't smart enough for university so I have to settle for this average career."

It's not only culture that implanted the "work hard to be successful and become somebody" notion — it's also our inner sensations and gratifications that come with small successes and the pain of failure. Being praised by our parents after getting an "A" for the first time at school confirms our feeling that success will make life good, more than any verbal teaching ever could.

We regard those who suffer, such as the poor, the homeless, and addicted, as the losers in life. Therefore, we naturally regard the rich and happy as the winners. The feeling of happiness, the sensation of spending money, and the moments when our desires are satisfied all reaffirm the deep belief rooted in our mind that life will be good once we become a millionaire or a "somebody". "I'm so happy to own a new Ford; imagine how happy I'd be to buy a new Mercedes!" This default, that life will be good when success is achieved, is near-universal across all levels of class in society, but is particularly strong in Western countries, where individualism is a more mainstream mentality.

Movies and TV programmes reinforce the concept: classic Disney movies always have a happy ending. In *Cinderella*, for example, Cinderella finally gets married to the prince and the last words are "they lived happily ever after". Cinderella's struggles in life are over and she is happy. Nobody doubts or bothers to think about Cinderella after her marriage, other than to assume that she and the prince "live happily ever after". Nobody stops to think that she may argue, fight with, or even divorce the prince. In most people's minds, arguments, fights, and divorce only happen to ordinary people, not successful people like Cinderella and her prince. In the minds of all the boys watching, their wish is to be a prince one day, marry a beauty like Cinderella, eventually become king, and live a happy, fantastic life. In a girl's mind, the wish is to be Cinderella and one day marry a prince so she can live happily ever after. Western popular culture repeats a similar message through all kinds of media every day, meaning the belief that success will equal happiness has become deep-rooted in our psyche.

However, the delusion of success doesn't mean that success is not good or not real. It means that the *presumption* that success will bring happiness is a delusion. Success — personal goals or ambitions — is, in itself, not bad or unreal. It's a pleasure to accomplish a goal and be successful. However, success itself cannot and will not solve all of our problems, no matter how grand the success appears to be. In fact, success can barely solve any of our main problems or fetters in life at all, save the fleeting moment of euphoria , like when a professional athlete wins their first grand championship.

Personal success is the realisation of our personal goals or ambitions. As we discussed when considering desires as fetters, personal goals are our desires. When our desires are satisfied, as in the case of success, we feel pleasure at the moment of satisfaction, but that is all. Personal success in professions or businesses cannot solve our conflicts with other people. Becoming CEO of a Fortune 500 company won't relieve us of worries or solve the problem of our child being addicted to drugs. Reaching the zenith of the art or sports world cannot make our insomnia any less painful. The list goes on and on. Any notions of "they lived happily ever after" are just wishful thinking. They are fantasies created by Hollywood to induce people to watch more of their movies, and they couldn't be further away from the realities of life.

Most people will live their entire lives ignorant of the fact that they are chasing the wind. We can live our whole life under such a delusion if we never achieve ultimate success. Ironically, on the day that we truly become the prince or Cinderella, we experience a crisis as the delusion of success bubble finally bursts. This is exactly what happens when people enter a mid-life crisis.

Mid-life crisis: The crisis of success!

Between the ages of 35 and 60, some people — particularly men — go through a period of crisis.[17,76,77] Quite often, men who have been successful in their careers suddenly lose interest in the job or profession they have always energetically pursued. They can become unhappy with their marriage or relationships and blame their wife or partner for their problems. They become resentful of everything in life but are confused why. They experience some of the worst emotions they've ever had and are deeply disappointed with the situations and surroundings they find themselves in, whether they're executive managers or housewives. Quite often, they ask self-reflecting questions such as "Is this what my life is?", "Why am I doing this?" or "What value does my job actually have?"

Such a crisis often starts after a milestone, like their youngest child grows up and buys their own home, or they get the promotion at work that they had sought for a long time. Instead of enjoying the satisfaction of accomplishment, they feel awkward and empty. They feel cheated by life, because instead of the happiness they dreamed would come with achieving their goals, they instead find hollowness and a sense of being trapped. They feel that in pursuing their goals, they missed out on a lot of fun. At that moment, they feel there must be more to life than what they've experienced so far, and they go looking for it. In what seems like revenge, they begin buying expensive cars, clothes, and holidays; they even cheat on their partners. However, in satisfying these desires, they find the same feeling of hollowness.

Women often experience mid-life crises differently to men. For women who follow the "traditional" female life pattern, as the so-called "caregiver" or "nurturer" of the family,[17] they may have a mid-life crisis when their children leave home and the role they filled changes. They might have given up a promising career and ambitions to look after the kids, despite being highly educated. When their children grow up and leave for university, they may feel empty, meaningless, and restless. Even if they are quite well-off financially, nothing can fill the vacuum created by the children leaving home. They may envy their husband for having a successful career and their kids for living lives full of excitement. They may feel left out, with a profound sense of hollowness and of not knowing what to do next.

Women who put their career success first can also have a mid-life crisis more akin to men. After they've reached their professional goals, they don't find the happiness they expected to. Instead, they feel discontented and depressed. They start to doubt their decision to not have kids or get married for the sake of a successful career. They may even enthusiastically pursue the traditional family lifestyle they disdained a few years before.[17]

Ironically, those hit hardest by mid-life crises are those who — in society's eyes — are the most successful. Some of them are true geniuses in their field, determined super-achievers who worked harder than anyone else to achieve their goals. They include the "wonder-kids" who overcame childhood adversity to climb to the top of their ladder. Success is written all over them; they may be married to gorgeous women, own big houses in the most exclusive parts of town, travel the world first-class, and go on luxury holidays. They may be respected and always at the centre of their business or social circles.

Similarly, the puzzling aspect of women leaving their husbands during their mid-life crisis is that most of them are economically well-off.[17] It's not poverty or the hardship of having to work a part-time job to make ends meet that drives some women to leave their homes. Instead, it's the feelings of meaningless, absurdity, and emptiness that bring too much pain for them to continue the status quo.[17]

The most ironic part about people suffering a mid-life crisis is that they themselves seem to feel that they have no reason to be unhappy! He's earned more money than he could ever dream of and exceeded his most ambitious expectations in a field he loves. She married a successful, loving husband and they live in a big house in a gated, upper-class, suburban community. They have healthy, well-behaved children. Yet they don't know why they're still not content. Surely it's ridiculous for them to be unhappy with life?! However, the sad reality is that they just feel awful and don't know what to do to change it.

What causes a mid-life crisis?

The question then is: what are the root causes of such mental pain at a time when these people are supposed to be enjoying their seemingly wonderful lives? Numerous theories have been suggested to explain mid-life crises, such as male-menopause,[76] a passage among many one has to pass in the cycle of life,[17] the fading of strength and youth,[78] a diminishing sex-drive, the first-time realisation of one's own mortality, a diminishing social and psychological status,[79] or the gradual disintegration of an identity formulated by culture and parents — leading to the discovery of an individual's authentic identity.[17] Some authors attribute it to our seeking the other, inner side of our psyche so we can become psychologically whole,[77] or to a search for our own true "self". Such theories refer to it as a "creative illness."[80]

All of these points are relevant to mid-life crises and make sense in understanding their causes to a certain degree and with some validity. However, they all miss the key issue: *the loss of goals in life in a mid-life crisis*.

A loss of goals and bursting the delusion of success bubble both occur when someone achieves success and reaches the summit of life. This is the only common character underlining all mid-life crises. It is also unique to mid-life crises, distinguishing them from other stressful periods in people's lives.

It's no surprise that people miss this, the most important characteristic of mid-life crises, due to the lack of understanding around the essence of success and the role of personal goals or ambitions in our lives. Without a clear understanding of the limits of success and the true role of goals, it's impossible to understand mid-life crises. As we've seen, most of our life experiences are sub-Flow processes. The goal of a sub-Flow process is its most crucial part. It's the decisive incentive that drives the whole process, providing meaning and context.[13]

Importantly, the process of achieving a goal forms the majority of an ordinary person's daily routine. In a sub-Flow process, although people may not enjoy the activities themselves as much as in a Flow activity, they do provide a task to focus on, allowing them to temporarily forget or put aside their troubles, providing a curtain that prevents them from confronting or being consumed by fetters. This is why people feel better at work than they do when staying at home doing nothing on Sunday, even if they don't enjoy their work at all. [13]

Work, or even household chores, provide some order for our mental activities and stop us falling victim to our unpredictable moods and chaotic thoughts.[13] Many people who keep themselves busy from project to project use work as a way of avoiding relationship troubles or inner turmoil;[17] it becomes a refuge from their problems. Therefore, even though work in general isn't as fun as entertainment, it provides us with a long period where we can focus our attention away from the conflicts in our life or our unmanageable mental fetters.

The idea that achieving our goals will provide us with everlasting happiness helps us to cope with daily life. As Viktor Frankl reiterated Nietzsche's saying, "He who has a why to live for can bear with almost any how".[81] We endure pain that others would find unbearable. We go through a boring routine of training day after day to become successful in future competitions and make it to the top of the podium. We push aside disappointments or mishaps to focus on important projects.

Such work enables us not to be overwhelmed and consumed by inevitable misfortunes. Instead, it forces us to focus on the things that need doing. Pain, conflicts, and disappointments are regarded as the price we have to pay, the sacrifice we have to make for the sake of our future success.

For many, work, jobs, or business are their only focus in life. They are so convinced that success means everything that all other aspects of their lives are deemed expendable. They neglect their health by working around the clock to meet deadlines. Even after their honeymoon or the birth of their first child, some people barely have five minutes for their partner or child because their goals are so important to them. When relationships begin to suffer, work, jobs, and projects become an even greater refuge from conflicts at home or inner troubles.

The goals of our life don't need to be very clear or consistent. In fact, very few people have clear and consistent goals as children that they accomplish as adults. Most of us only have a vague idea of the person we want to become. Usually, we're drifting along on the tide of time, gradually forming our goals, changing and adapting them with every passing year.

Influenced by our parents as children, we might aim to become a scientist — only to find that our science and maths skills aren't strong enough. Thus, we'll naturally shift our goals to other areas such as arts, business, or social sciences. We might have dreamed of becoming a doctor but found medical training too intense and expensive, so we settled for another job instead. Trying to survive and prosper in our time and environment, we modify our goals to fit changes in the needs or demands of society.

We pursue certain careers when there are good job prospects for them. We upgrade our goals when we find unexpected success. For example, we may originally have aimed to find a decent job in a new field but soon climbed to the top of a fast-growing company. Likewise, we downscale our goals when we fumble, failing the entrance exam for a prestigious university for example. We change our goals many times before we finally settle on the career or job we take as means to make a living. Despite that, our goals — no matter how clear and ambitious or vague and insignificant to others — always seem to promise us a better future, enticing us to go through the inevitable pain and suffering in life.

However, that goal, which has driven us along this tedious road for so many years, suddenly disappears when we reach success. For most of us, that doesn't entail scoring a last-minute winner live on TV. It's more likely that we've reached the highest rung on the corporate ladder or achieved the highest status we can in our profession or company. We might have been made partner of a prestigious law firm or developed a successful small business but have no further ambitions. Consciously or subconsciously, we know that we've reached the summit, the highest point of our life's journey.

Instead of the champagne-filled celebration we dreamed of, we arrive at the summit of our life with an unbelievably plain feeling. The first reaction is disbelief: *is this it?* Whither the glory and grandness? The reality is a complete let-down. We climb this slippery mountain for years, enduring hardship and pain, making so many sacrifices for the promise of the view from the top. Instead, we see office blocks on the other side of the street, the same ones we've been looking at for decades, with an even clearer view of their ugliness. Where is the happiness promised to us? Where is the contentment?

The mirage is shattered to pieces ruthlessly right in front of us. The higher and more complete our success is, the harder the let-down. It's the most successful people who experience the worst mid-life crises, as their delusions cannot continue. At least the vice-president of a company might still have the delusion of a better life if he could reach the very top. The CEO has no such chance of delusion.

Theoretically, everyone has to pass over a "summit" in life. However, only those at the highest level — managers, professionals, artists, and entrepreneurs — will have a distinct sense of self-realisation that they reached the "top". A traditionally trained tradesperson has such a clearly defined career path that they won't have any unrealistic expectations or ambitions. Their experience of the top would feel more like a plateau than a summit. They might experience a lot of stress in life, but would not have that distinctive realisation of reaching the top.

The vast majority of average salary workers, blue-collars, or non-managerial white-collars go through a similar experience. From a young age, through a lack of adequate education or other limitations, they had no great ambitions. They may experience more stress than those who are more successful, but their experience of the top of life is not much worse than other periods in their life.

Only those who reach obvious success have the chance to experience the clear and distinctive internal reactions to the bubble of delusion bursting. This is the main reason why even in the United States, only about 10% of the population show clear symptoms of a mid-life crisis.[82] There would be no disappointment if there was no expectation in the first place. The greater the expectation, the greater the disappointment.

The more we believe in the dream, the harder we chase it, the more heartbroken we'll be after. After the initial disbelief, people suffering a mid-life crisis experience deep remorse and self-pity, particularly those who've grossly neglected their family's needs in their single-minded pursuit of success. And there is resentment, bitter resentment; we feel cheated by those who influenced the decisions we made as youngsters that now leave us feeling trapped. We resent our partners, children, and families for the obligations and financial burdens they place on us, making it impossible for us to start anew. We become hostile towards our bosses and co-workers for all the hardships we have to deal with in our work.

Life becomes meaningless during a mid-life crisis, and this is one of its worst aspects. "Why am I doing this?" and "Why do I sell others bullshit I no longer believe in?" All the hardships we've endured become absurd to us. We've been imagining all this time that life will be better when we become successful, that our problems will go away when our business takes off. Now, here we are. Success. But this external success only brings the realisation of failure. If such wretchedness is all it brings, what is the meaning of success? It seems absurd to continue living this way, chasing the wind.

The collective mid-life crisis

Existentialism is a philosophy that hails from a time when humanity faced a collective mid-life crisis. Refusing to accept the goals, meaning, and values provided by traditional religion, modern philosophers from the Renaissance onwards have tried hard to figure out a secular meaning for human life but have always failed. Existentialism's cry of "no goal, no meaning, and no value for human existence" — an existential crisis — is a dilemma still haunting humanity today despite glorious material successes in science and technology.

Nietzsche's desperate cries of "he who has a why to live for can bear with almost any how" [81] and "Absurd! Absurd! Absurd!" still apply to those who no longer have a goal in life. Jean-Paul Sartre's quote "life has no meaning the moment you lose the illusion of being eternal" accurately describes the similar, desperate cry from those in the midst of a mid-life crisis.

Without a goal in life, we're trapped in whatever circumstances we find ourselves in. The trouble is we don't know how to break free of this trap. Nothing prepares us for this sudden storm in the middle of our lives, far less what to do after it. In all the scripts, the story ends when Cinderella marries the prince. The struggle is over. We live happily ever after with all of our accomplishments, sitting leisurely, watching all the people still busy trying to be as successful as we are. But we're nowhere near. We're in limbo, big time, suspended in mid-air without any clue how or when we can break out.

A lack of goals

The Sunday morning blues (the worst mood conditions observed by Csikszentmihalyi in his research when people do not go to church and have nothing to do at home on Sundays[13]) strike people when they have no goal, which means no meaning for their activities on a Sunday morning. However, the Sunday morning blues are bearable because they're only one day per week. People know, even if only subconsciously, that they have work the following day, making the rest of the week more meaningful. Although they may not realise it, it's much easier for people to beat the Sunday morning blues when meaningful work awaits them in the not-too-distant future. One morning of the blues is bad enough — imagine how terrible it would be to suffer them for years! The Sunday morning blues are a taste of what a mid-life crisis feels like.

Many of us probably experience them or something similar before we enter mid-life. It happens during the period when we accomplish one goal but have yet to set another: when we graduate from college and are unsure whether to work, travel, or study further. Such times are challenging to us and we feel awkward, anxious, and restless, even if we've done well in our studies. We don't find relief until we settle on our next plan of action.

Such episodes are common in life, from our school years onwards, but they normally only last a few days or weeks at the most, until we find our next goal. A mid-life crisis is different. We've reached the summit, the ultimate goal we've been dreaming of since childhood. There are no more rungs left on the ladder. We can't even share our troubles with others, because who would believe us with all of our success? What is wrong with us? What mistakes have led us into this dead end? Where do we go from here? We get no answer.

A person suffering a mid-life crisis is consumed by this endless internal trial day and night. It may assume different forms: mental disturbances, depression, neurosis, psycho-physical malfunctions, or psychoses, all of which cause internal pain. These people lose interest in the outside world, absorbed in internal dialogues, reflections, and contemplation.

Stressors in mid-life crises are the same or similar to those experienced earlier in life, at least in other people's eyes.[83] This is one of the main reasons why some researchers doubt the existence of the mid-life crisis.[82]

Yet the stressors appear bigger and more intense than before. Without the mask of a goal, we're forced to face reality's naked ugliness. The troubles in our lives are magnified, their magnitudes doubling.

In the past, we served and tolerated those we hated for good reasons, such as for the sake of our careers. But when our concern for success is gone, we lack such restraint. We're less tolerant of and more hostile to our colleagues and spouses. In the past, we tried to avoid confrontation by escaping into our work. We regarded any family problems at home as a part of life, one we could leave on the back-burner whilst we occupied ourselves with our careers. Now, without the refuge of a job that needs focus to occupy our mind, we nit-pick about others, blaming them for the weight of responsibility on our shoulders.

Yet the most punishing aspect of a mid-life crisis is our confrontation with the inner reality of the self and the demons inside us. Most of the negative emotions, chaotic thoughts, and excessive desires we think are caused by other people or events actually originate within us. Without a goal in the external world to strive for, we're forced to confront the reality of our inner self head-on, involuntarily dwelling on it for hours.

We find that the roots of the battles we've been fighting in the external world all these years, which have caused us so much pain, are inside us; they *are* us! The anxiety we thought was caused by external stress is, in reality, an integral part of ourselves. Anger at family, co-workers, the news, society, the whole world… all of it is rooted within us.

We're at the mercy of our inner demons without the help of something deviating our attention from the outside world. The worst part of it is that we have no idea how to fight these inner demons. We may have won all kinds of battles in the external world, but these demons are much more confusing.

We use alcohol and other substances for relief, even temporarily. We'll try anything: sexual promiscuity, bungee-jumping, rock climbing... the more audacious and risky the adventure, the better, because it's more likely to divert our attention and focus from our internal turmoil. However, the euphoria or escape induced by alcohol and drugs is short-lived and leaves us with even more guilt and disappointment. All of this can easily lead to the misery of severe depression or even suicide, the rates of which are exceptionally high in middle-aged men.[17]

Who is spared?

Thankfully, as recent research has shown, not everyone has to go through the misery of a mid-life crisis.[82] So, who is spared, even after they've achieved their goals?

Firstly, as we've seen, mid-life crises are borne out of a lack of goals once we've achieved everything we set out to do. Ironically, it's only because personal success is so widespread in economically developed societies that mid-life crises are a common phenomenon to begin with.

Secondly, for a mid-life crisis to happen, people must regard personal goals as the ultimate goals in life and individualism must be accepted as a societal standard, which is the case in most Western countries today. Where the majority of the population is struggling for survival, there is no room for mid-life crises. This is why mid-life crises are seldom mentioned in historical literature, save for a few individual cases. [84] During hard times, which form most of human history, the vast majority of people focused on day-to-day survival; there was no chance for them to feel they'd reached success.

There is no shortage of goals in life when a country is at war or when basic resources are scarce. This is the case for most people today, particularly those in third world countries where poverty is widespread and basic survival needs are barely met. Most people are simply struggling to survive poverty, the evils of tyrannical dictatorship, epidemics, etc. In such situations, the aims or goals of life are very clear: to put enough food on the table, to keep warm, and to care for family members who are sick. The list of challenges that the external world provides can be overwhelming; there's no time for indulging in individual success.

In a rich country such as the USA, where individual accomplishment is a mainstream goal for people, a mid-life crisis is still not inevitable. The first group of people who wouldn't fall into such a trap are those whose life goals are bigger than their personal ones, those whose aspirations benefit wider society above themselves.

Mother Teresa, Martin Luther King, Nelson Mandela, and Abraham Lincoln belong to this group. The aspirations or goals they sought in life were (and remain) vast and never-ending. They may have achieved intermediate success, but they seldom reached their ultimate goal. When alleviating the suffering of the poorest of the poor in the ghettos of India, Mother Teresa never encountered a day when she could feel she'd finished her mission, that there was no goal left for her to strive for. She died in the middle of that perpetual calling, and she could never have found a moment to experience a mid-life crisis.

People with a calling in life don't need to be as rare and heroic as those mentioned here though. They can be anyone with a deep conviction for an aspiration bigger than them, who applies that conviction as the main task in their lives — be it animal welfare advocates, environmentalists, or those who devote their free time to community causes — all of them belong to this mid-life crisis-free group. They could be anyone, of any rank, at any level of society. All that differentiates them from the rest of the population is that deep down, they have the conviction for goals bigger than themselves in life.

However, working for a charity, a non-profit organisation, or even in a prominent position cannot guarantee exemption from a mid-life crisis. As long as people feel deep inside their mind that personal ambitions such as a big salary, power, being "someone", or having a successful career are the main motivation, then a mid-life crisis is possible. The same is true for many of the pastors working in churches who regard preaching as more of a job, career, or profession than their soul's answer to God's calling.[79]

On the other hand, if someone works in a for-profit organisation or government body but has a strong motivation to serve others, they will most likely avoid a mid-life crisis. For example, janitors who proudly look after a building. There's always something higher to aim for when the goal is to serve others above oneself. Despite that, it's important to note that even those with a calling in life aren't immune to many of life's crises, such as depression. Remember that difficulties, troubles, challenges, and crises are all fetters and may occur to anyone at any stage of their life.

If someone with a calling is experiencing turmoil, don't doubt their sincerity. For example, Abraham Lincoln was consumed with the daunting task of leading America at a critical junction of history, his calling, but he wasn't spared the depressive effects of a melancholy character and a tough marriage. Likewise, Mother Teresa experienced doubts and struggles over her religious beliefs, which lasted most of her life.[85]

Finally, it's worth noting that in reality, few of us are pure angels and few are wholly self-centred. The vast majority of us are a mix of both in varying degrees. The key point is that the more we're occupied with our individual goals, the more likely we are to have a mid-life crisis. And the more we see success as a pinnacle to be reached, the more we'll struggle when we get there.

The second group of people who will be spared a mid-life crisis are those who see processes instead of results as their goals in life. These are people who have many Flow experiences. They are the lucky ones who make a living doing the things they love, even without pay. The music teacher who loves music and teaching; the computer geek who loves troubleshooting and can make a living as a technician. Such people won't suffer a mid-life crisis because they love the process itself. They aren't lured in by the pay, or at least it's not their main motivation. To these people, the process itself is the main focus, and everything else is secondary.

A professional athlete is a typical example of this group of people. As long as professional athletes truly love and enjoy their chosen sport, they will never encounter a mid-life crisis as we know it. However, when a professional athlete has lost their genuine interest in the game and the pay and fame become the main motivation, they are no longer immune to a mid-life crisis, no matter how many millions they earn or how famous they are.

However, the largest group of people who don't experience mid-life crises, or at least experience it to a lesser extent, are those who haven't yet reached their goals in life and are still pursuing money and success. Hundreds of millions, even billions, of people live their everyday life this way, without realising that they're living a delusion. Millions of people in second- or third-world countries envy the comfort and luxury that people in first-world countries enjoy. Those who are poor or live a mediocre life, such as the middle class in first-world countries, wish they led more lavish, glamorous lifestyles.

As long as people are still pursuing their dreams, they won't encounter a mid-life crisis. Even most of those who are already truly successful, the rich and famous people on our televisions, are often completely unaware that they're pursuing a delusion. They are the people who regard winning as the be-all and end-all in life. Despite making hundreds of millions, more money is still their goal and there will never be enough for them.

These people conduct their lives like kids addicted to video games; they just want to win. The difference is that kids are aware the characters in the game are unreal and that it's only a game, whereas rich people in society and business are deadly serious about their games and play them wholeheartedly. The big games of businesses and state affairs can affect not just the well-being of those playing them but millions of other real people in society too.

Moreover, when kids play video games, their parents or guardians will remind them and even discipline them from time to time so they don't indulge themselves too much in these games. In big business games, however, there are no parents or guardians to sanction someone's behaviour. Instead, there are only envious stares from the rest of the world, who are just as delusional. This only heightens a business person's pursuit of success, even though they never truly enjoy the process of their games as much as kids playing their favourite video games; cursing and venting profanely at their subordinates and co-workers as they struggle to win.

They roll up their sleeves every day and fight against their competitors with all the energy they can muster from their aching bodies. It's like they're under a spell. In their zombie-like mindset, religious teachings are for the weak, morals and ethics are laughable — mere hurdles for them to overcome in convincing others to follow suit. Even laws and the consequences of breaking them are simple inconveniences, and they're not reluctant to break these laws if they believe they can get away with it.

The world has been under this spell for a long time and is still under its tight grip today. Not only in America but in China and other emerging countries too, from the elites to the factory floor. The spell is so pervasive that even monks and pastors in temples and churches, whose role in society is to remind us of the futility of material success, are just as delusional as the rest. They wholeheartedly engage themselves in the business of spirituality, enjoying their prosperity when patrons' alms fill their donation buckets.

The world is truly a farce when such pretentious mumbling monks and ostentatious gurus, wrapped in the most colourful and lavish clothing imaginable, conduct their preaching when their true purpose is nothing but the same delusion of money, success, and fame that misleads the rest of us. There is no hope of salvation if we cannot liberate ourselves from the slavery of this spell.

There is no hope for humanity in delusions and no hope of true happiness in pursuing money and success, no matter how grand. As lamented by a certain Donald Trump in his book *Surviving at the Top,* "To be always moving toward a new goal—if that's not the key to happiness, then it's the key to achieve a state that's as close to happiness as you're going to get in this life."[86]

We'll have a better idea of the liberation and salvation waiting for those in the middle of a mid-life crisis in the next. But the whole picture will be revealed in the next book in this series, *How to Obtain Happiness and Why.*

The hidden blessing

Despite all of this, there is a potential blessing in a mid-life crisis! Millions could accuse me of sarcasm here.

A caterpillar transforming into a butterfly is an apt metaphor for a mid-life crisis. Caterpillars have to go through the pupa stage to become butterflies. Without this stage, during which they are incarcerated and immobile in cocoons and in great danger of becoming food for many predators, caterpillars are unable to reach their final stage of being a butterfly, enjoying the freedom of flight. Mid-life crises can be understood as a pupa stage for humans, moving them towards liberty and salvation, the destiny of human life.

A mid-life crisis is a painful awakening in the middle of our delusional dreams. It's a forced paradigm shift, reserved only for those lucky enough to have reached ultimate success in an otherwise mundane life. Being trapped in the cocoon is painful. There are many dangers of becoming food for predators: alcoholism, drug addiction, depression, and even suicide. However, there's also the chance of triumph, of emerging from the crisis with an unfaltering conviction regarding one's purpose and goals for the rest of their life.

Mid-life crises in other cultures

As the root cause of mid-life crises is the loss of goals after achieving success, this can explain why they seldom happen in Japanese or Indian cultures. In Western culture, or the prevalent mainstream hedonistic culture of today's world, personal interest is placed at the centre of life and individualism is the true belief of people, even those who regard themselves as religious. We are viewed and judged, both by ourselves and others, on how much money we make, how successful we are, how famous we become, or how much power we can leverage. Personal success and individual accomplishment are the natural, unquestioned goals of life.

However, in traditional Japanese culture, [56] individualism is almost regarded as a sin and is scorned, particularly when the individual is but one member of a big organisation. From an early stage, children are taught by their parents and teachers to be a good group member, be liked by everyone in the group, and not to offend others. The focus is always on the success of the whole organisation, not any specific individual, even if the individual plays an extremely important role in the organisation's success. When important decisions are made, even with a leader at the helm, they're collective decisions with thorough consultation and feedback, or at least that's the ideal. Both the glory of success and humiliation of failure lie on the whole group instead of the individual at the top.[56]

Furthermore, career advancement and pay depend largely on seniority rather than individual merit. People seldom jump between companies to advance their careers, a common practice in corporate America. In corporate Japan, a person rarely reaches the top of their career until just before retirement. Both the downplay of individualism in Japanese culture and the fact that almost no one has reached the peak of success in middle-age results in the almost non-existence of mid-life crises in Japan.

However, Japanese people do experience similar crises, only after retirement. The "company men", those who have devoted their whole lives to the company they worked for, know nothing else and are interested in nothing else. This group reportedly have extreme difficulty after retirement because they have lost their goals and subsequently lost any meaning in their lives. Even their wives encounter a unique Japanese mental problem, "retired husband syndrome", a crisis of being companions to such men. [87]

In traditional Indian culture, it's also rare for people to be found experiencing a mid-life crisis. However, this is caused by different factors than in Japanese culture. There are at least three reasons why mid-life crises are less prevalent in traditional Indian culture than in Western societies.

Firstly, India is still a developing country with a per capita income (nominal) of $1670 per year in 2016, ranked at 112th out of 164 countries by the World Bank.[88] When people are still struggling for basic needs, there's little chance for them to feel that their life has no goals.

Secondly, in traditional Indian culture, it's common for big families with three or more generations to live together in the same house. Even though today's family sizes are smaller than in the past, the family is still a prominent part of modern Indian society. In other countries where multiple generations of family members live together, the older generation often lives with only one of their sons or daughters. In traditional Indian families, married brothers with their own children live together under the supervision of the Karta, usually the oldest member of the family.

This unique setting and culture of family life downplays the impact and importance of personal success or accomplishment. When a person reaches a prominent status in society, such as becoming rich or famous, the whole family is proud of the success and benefits from it. When a big income makes it possible for the whole extended family to enjoy good lifestyle and they're grateful for it, the success doesn't feel meaningless or the hard work empty.

There is another factor for the relative absence of mid-life crises in Indian society: the importance of spirituality. Traditionally, all aspects of Indian culture and civilisation were created from, and revolve around, its religions and spirituality. Even today, Brahmins are regarded as the highest members of society.

The mundanity of life, hardship, and success are regarded as secondary in the minds of many Indians. It's accepted that material riches won't bring fulfilment because, to paraphrase Buddhism, everything is empty after all. When you become rich and successful, you're given an opportunity to perform charity, to give the money away to the poor. Multi-nationals in India such as Tata Group are owned mainly by trusts, with charity as their mission. In 2011, India mandated by law that companies above a certain size are required to donate 2% of their annual profit to charity.

In fact, we can see that a mid-life crisis results from the loss of goals in life after reaching personal success when we consider the increase in mid-life crises among a particular group of people in India — those who are exceptionally successful and become rich at a young age. These are the "new money" people who have often made their fortune in the IT industry and have embraced materialism and individualism over traditional Indian values and culture. It was reported that people in the Indian IT industry younger than 35 have been diagnosed with symptoms similar to a mid-life crisis.[89]

When a person truly believes in personal successes and achieves it, the trap of a mid-life crisis awaits. But when personal success or accomplishments are seen as means to achieving higher goals for everyone, rather than the ultimate individual goal of a person's life, then a mid-life crisis can be avoided. You won't feel that there are no more goals to strive for in life once you've achieved success if you see it as something bigger than yourself, as your calling for humanity.

CHAPTER 8:

Quantifying Happiness

Since Jeremy Bentham, social scientists (particularly economists) have made serious efforts to quantify the pleasure, well-being, or happiness of mankind. In the past few decades, significant efforts have been made by some countries and international bodies as well as individual researchers to design many indices such as the Human Development Index (HDI)[18] to reflect the overall well-being of humans as individuals and as a group. In this chapter, we will consider the various ways that humans have attempted to quantify happiness and propose a new method of quantification. Feel free to skip the calculations if this part is not relevant to you.

Theories of happiness quantification

To the disappointment of most researchers, there's still no viable index that can quantify the well-being or happiness of a society or a country as easily as GDP does, which is recognised by most as grossly inadequate in quantifying the true well-being or happiness of individuals or as a country. As early utilitarians found, pleasures are next to impossible to quantify due to their unlimited varieties and the incompatibility between different pleasures (eating a favourite cookie and reading an inspiring book, for example). Modern-day equivalents of utilitarianism, such as subjective well-being, don't fare much better in their attempts.[18] The trouble with trying to assess global happiness or global life satisfaction is that — other than to what degree people are happy or satisfied with their lives — we know little about why people feel that they feel it.

Other methods have attempted to quantify happiness by combining indices.[18,90] One such attempt, Gross National Happiness (GNH), seems to take a holistic approach towards notions of progress and gives equal importance to non-economic aspects of well-being.[90,91] In the GNH Index, for example, 33 indicators are categorised under nine domains to reflect the overall well-being of the people of Bhutan (where the index originates from). The nine domains include standard of living, health, education, time use, good governance, ecological diversity and resilience, psychological well-being, community vitality, cultural diversity, and resilience.

There is no question that GNH is much better than GDP at reflecting overall well-being. However, in addition to the subjective nature of its indicator choice and poor compatibility between different countries, there are some fundamental shortfalls with GNH. The happiness or well-being that people feel is immensely diverse and personal. The fixed indicators and corresponding weights of GNH can be grossly inadequate in measuring the true well-being of an individual. I call this a lack of "genuineness" in the index.

Genuineness is different from the subjectivity or objectivity that concerns researchers in natural or social sciences. In the field of happiness study, we are concerned with how people feel and how they evaluate their life experiences, both of which are inherently subjective. Thus, subjective questions and answers in any surveys or index are just as important as objective ones, if not more. The key to a useful survey or index of happiness is not about how subjective or objective it is but how genuine or authentic it is in reflecting the true feeling, conditions, or status of the people surveyed. The fundamental question regarding the genuineness of GNH is whether 33 indicators and over 120 questions truly reflect the happiness of the people of Bhutan? The simple answer is no.

GNH's shortfalls are best illustrated by examples. Imagine a senior citizen who is ridden with serious health conditions such as severe arthritis or late-stage cancer. For such a man, physical health is extremely important in the overall quality of his life, due to his age and the severity of his conditions. His health is so bad that he is bed-ridden and in constant pain. Suppose this senior also has a good income and excellent relationships with others. Physical health aside, he is very positive, open, and optimistic to the point that he could achieve a near-perfect GNH score. Thus, from the GNH score, he should be one of the happiest people surveyed. But in reality, he is anything but happy with his physical conditions. The pain could be so bad that he might welcome death as a release. This is, of course, an extreme example, but it shows how misleading a happiness survey can be.

Yet, the biggest problem of indices, which makes them un-genuine, is how the weighting is assigned to every domain, category, and question. As we saw in our example of the imaginary senior, their score is untrue in reflecting their actual situation to some degree. Such un-genuineness is standard in any happiness indices reliant on domain happiness or life satisfaction (such as a job, family, relationship, etc.)[18] It exists in the majority of people to varying degrees: a blue-collar worker in a small, predominantly white, Republican-voting town in southern America is less likely to give a damn about ecological diversity and resilience or culture diversity and resilience than someone living in a more cosmopolitan metropolis. Thus, these two categories are irrelevant to them.

The fundamental challenge for any method to construe overall, global happiness from domain happiness (or a single question) is the fact that we experience life in every moment through a comprehensive awareness combination (a tribunal of four to five levels of awareness). Which level of awareness dominates a person's life at any given moment (and thus will be felt as a life experience at that moment) is a dynamic fluid equilibrium that is forever changing. None of us experiences a formulaic life in a day, say: 10% in the financial aspect of life; 30% in the work-related aspect; 10% in the family-related aspect, and 35% in physical or mental health. Thus it is impossible to formulate an index to calculate one individual's overall life experiences from a set of domains with arbitrarily assigned weight ratios, let alone measure a population's.

As we observe in our own lives, the issues concerning human life and happiness are incredibly individual. A late-stage cancer patient's life concerns are vastly different from those of a teenage girl who is the victim of bullying at school. Irrelevant categories or questions and the arbitrary weights given to them are the main reasons why GNH cannot truly calculate happiness of people of Bhutan or the world.

A new way to quantify happiness

As we have seen, how people feel about their life and how happy they are depends more on the fetters in their lives than the pleasure afforded by the temporary satisfaction of desires. Compared with the dominant effect of fetters on our daily life, the effects of pleasure or other seemingly random events are almost negligible. Pleasure is also relative and brings inherent suffering when the desire it provokes can't be immediately satisfied, whether it's an alcoholic who can't get a drink or a sports fan whose team is losing. The downside of desire cancels out the positive side that a pleasure may bring.

What's more, the fulfilment of one desire will still leave another ten unfulfilled, as Schopenhauer pointed out two centuries ago. [16] In today's society, with its barrage of advertising, emphasis on materialism, and stagnant wage growth, there may be twenty desires that have to be denied so that one desire can be fulfilled. There are so many extravagances out there that the satisfaction of regular things in our daily life always seems so insignificant. Desires and wants last a long time, but satisfaction is just a fleeting moment. Lacking and longing are the norms of life, and unsatisfaction and discontent are both inevitable and constant.

Therefore, instead of counting the moments or number of pleasures we have in life, as suggested by utilitarianism or hedonism, we can regard pleasures as almost irrelevant in calculating happiness.

It's my opinion that any calculation of happiness has to account for factors that have major and significant effects on our well-being. Fetters are the dominant factors that affect every minute of our life. The more fetters we have and the more severe they are, the less happy we will be. Thus, the happiness equation suggested in this theory is:

$$H = 1 / \Sigma \, S_i F_i \qquad \qquad \text{Equation } \mathbf{8.1}$$

Where

H is happiness

F_i is the fetter number i of the person

S_i is the severity coefficient of the fetter i

Σ is the summation of all $S_i F_i$

The happiness of an individual is, therefore, a reciprocal of all their fetters with the severity coefficient combined.

This equation applies to the calculation of an individual's happiness.

When calculating a group of people such as a community or a country the equation should be:

Average H= [Σ {1/ Σ SiFi}n]/N   **Equation** 8.2

Where

Average H is the average happiness of the group

   Fi is the fetter number i of the person in the group

   Si is the severity coefficient of the fetter i

   n is the individual "**n**" in the group with the total number of "**N**"

   Σ is the summation

Unlike assessing happiness in an index such as GNH, this equation has no fixed or limited number of domains, categories, or questions arbitrarily chosen by researchers in the happiness equation. Instead, what constitutes fetters, their number, and severity are all decided and determined by the individual who, strictly speaking, is the only one who knows their true feelings.

Each individual has a unique happiness equation that will cover their well-being in material conditions and the macro and microenvironments of their life, but more importantly, it will also reveal aspects of inner well-being such as physical and mental health. The fetters included will tell the true story, the genuineness of someone's life conditions and life experiences.

Different people have different fetters in their lives that determine how they feel about themselves and how happy they are. The fetters of both an individual and a group can be measured in terms of number and severity.

The number of fetters is the first aspect of the happiness equation. The fewer fetters a person or a group of people have in their lives, the happier that person or group will be. The second aspect is the severity coefficient (Si) that affects the level of our happiness more prominently than the number of fetters. Si is determined by both the intensity and frequency of a fetter. The stronger the fetter and the more often we suffer from it, the higher the Si.

We all experience some physical pains in our daily life, minor cuts and bruises; small nuisances that will barely affect our day. However, if we break a leg, the excruciating pain is hard to bear and can severely affect our sense of happiness for days, weeks, months, or even years. As human beings, we also experience some sad things in life, small or big, from losing a game to losing a pet to losing a family member. We feel sad when we remember missed loved ones. Yet, such sad episodes will generally become fewer and easier with time, particularly if we get a new pet or meet new people.

These less intense cases of sadness are a far cry from the onset of severe depression, where a person is lost in an ocean of deep sadness. Day and night, the mentally ill feel nothing but sad, guilty, and angry without a moment's relief and without hope of a better tomorrow. Si reflects the different frequencies and intensities of fetters. The effect on our life of a fetter that occurs once every ten years is as day is to night when compared to omnipresent severe depression. Depression often haunts the mentally ill through insomnia, which is as bad as the unrelenting sadness or guilt felt during the day. Thus, quantitatively, Si is a function of both the intensity factor $fi(I)$ ($fi(I)$ is defined as the intensity factor of fetter i and frequency factor fi (R) (fi (R) is defined as the frequency factor of fetter i). So, Si of fetter i is:

$$Si=S\{fi(I), fi(R)\} \hspace{2cm} \text{Equation } \mathbf{8.3}$$

(**#:** Here "**R**" instead of "**F**" is used to represent frequency to avoid confusion with the symbol of fetter — "**F**" in Equation 8.1; 8.2)

How to correlate $fi(I)$, $fi(R)$, with Si, and eventually to **H** (happiness) to truly reflect the happiness of a person needs serious investigation, and one simple formula suggested here is:

$$Si=fi(I) \times fi(R) \hspace{2cm} \text{Equation } \mathbf{8.4}$$

One scale of $f(I)$ could be a number from "0", which indicates that the person is not bothered by the fetter at all, to "10", which indicates that the fetter is so strong that it's unbearable.

Similarly, one scale of $f(R)$ could be a number from "0", which indicates that the person is never bothered by the fetter, to "10", which indicates the omnipresence of the fetter.

Thus, with the formula of equation 8.4 and the scales of both f(**I**) and f(**R**) from 0 to 10, we have a combined measurement from "0" to "100" to differentiate the severity of a fetter in a person's life.

With the assignment of a number from "0" to "10" for both intensity factor f(I) and frequency factor f(R), the happiness measured in equation 8.1 for the vast majority of people would be less than 1. To display the distribution of happiness better among a population, we could multiply the happiness amount measured in equation 8.1 by a factor of 1,000 to normalise **H**, so:

$$H = 1000 \times 1/\Sigma\ S_iF_i$$

$$H = 1000 \times 1/\Sigma\ (f_i(\mathbf{I}) \times f_i(\mathbf{R})F_i) \qquad \text{Equation 8.5}$$

For a group of people such as a nation, then, the average normalised happiness will be:

$$Average\ H = \mathbf{1000} \times [\Sigma\ \{1/\Sigma\ SiFi\}n]/N$$

$$= 1000 \times [\Sigma\ \{1/\Sigma\ (f_i(\mathbf{I}) \times f_i(\mathbf{R})Fi)\}n]/N$$

$$\text{Equation 8.6}$$

Equation **8.5** could be applied to an individual at any time or for any duration within their lifespan, as both f$_i$(**I**) and f$_i$(**R**) change with time. It can reflect a person's happiness from moment to moment as well as their happiness in a given hour, day, month, year, or even in a lifetime.

When measuring or considering our happiness in a moment, we only need to see whether we are in a moment of pleasure or a negative experience. When we're having a good time, how good we feel depends on how intense our interest is in the activity we're doing, which in turn determines how fully the pleasure is masking fetters from our consciousness. When we're having a bad time, we're mainly occupied by the negative emotion felt at that moment. The condition, or our feeling in that moment, is determined mainly by how strongly we're feeling the negative emotion. It could be a trivial annoyance such as hitting nothing but red lights when driving to work or a rage that makes our blood boil.

When we're totally devoured by anger, the $fi(\mathbf{I})$ of the fetter is at its maximum and we have almost zero happiness. At the other end, when we're in a moment of euphoria, all of our troubles are outside our mind; all our fetters are gone in that moment and we have the happiness value of infinite (from equation 8.5). Between these two extremes, we live most of our lives. Extreme emotions of both positive and negative such as rages or euphoria are rare.

Equation 8.5 and equation 8.6 are equally valid in assessing our overall well-being during any period of our life because they can be applied to any moment. To calculate the average happiness of an hour, day, month, or year, we first need to identify what the main fetters of the period are. We can then assign both $fi(\mathbf{R})$ and $fi(\mathbf{I})$ to the fetter from our own life experience and feeling. Fetters are more stable and consistent than the elusive and ever-changing "good feeling" of pleasures. We know our problems like we know the fingers on our hand; they're so clear and overwhelming.

One advantage of measuring happiness by fetters and their corresponding severity coefficients being assigned by the host is that it can truly reflect how the person perceives the fetter concerned or the genuineness of their life lived. The impacts of an issue vary depending on individual conditions, particularly their perception of it. For example, losing £20 is a big thing in the life of someone struggling for money and they might spend the whole day being pissed off about it. But a busy billionaire who loses the same amount of money will probably not notice. Similarly, a certain noise may not affect a sound sleeper at all but could be a nightmare to a severe insomnia sufferer.

This is why in happiness economy, objective statistics don't always deliver a genuine picture, presenting instead a perceived vision (which no matter how twisted in the eyes of bystanders) is the reality seen by the host. The fetters and their importance, when measured in their corresponding severity coefficients, provide a "genuine" picture of how lives are lived.

The happiness measured in equation 8.5 reflects the true happiness of a person's lifetime, from birth until death, instead of just the period that a person is capable of rational reasoning, as is a prerequisite of other happiness indices such as GNH. It's impossible to measure a baby's happiness by asking the baby to answer 120 questions, so babies and other people below the age of adulthood are naturally excluded in the calculation of GNH and most other happiness surveys. However, we could measure the happiness of these people with reasonable accuracy by observing and calculating the fetters in their lives.

Children have less fetters in life than adults in general. Main fetters in an adult's life, such as worry, obligations, crisis, disasters, and negative emotions that burden adults so heavily aren't in the realm of childhood. As parents, we deliberately keep these inevitable fetters away from our children for the sake of their happiness. For example, most of us try not to break a child's naïve belief in Santa Claus too early. The health conditions of children generally are much better than adults except few who have severe conditions such as leukaemia or autism. When a child's family is above the poverty line, then social fetters or lack of adequate positive interactions are the main factors we need to look into when calculating the child's happiness.

For seniors who have lost their faculty of reasoning through dementia or other degenerative illnesses, regular happiness surveys are incapable of measuring their level of happiness either, meaning they're omitted from the statistics. However, equation 8.6 could reasonably reflect their happiness using the observations of their caregivers.

Equation 8.6 will be able to calculate the happiness of all people in a society, including those incapable of participating in regular happiness surveys such as those who have IQ scores well below-average that they cannot answer survey questions rationally. The fetters or challenges facing a person born with, say, Down's syndrome could be known to their parents or carers reasonably well.

The happiness equations of this theory can apply to any person in any culture or environment in any part of the world. This solves one of the biggest challenges in designing a universal happiness index (such as GNH). As we can observe in different parts of the world, people's preferences, likes and dislikes, and values are all different and are affected by the culture and the environment they were born into and grew up with.

Compared to past evaluation methods of happiness (such as Bentham's utility) or other current methods to measure levels of happiness such as various approaches in quantifying subjective-well-being, [18] the method proposed here can be called "negatively evaluated happiness". Almost all other evaluation methods used in various indices and surveys in mainstream happiness research focus on and measure how good the positive side of life is. The method advocated by this theory focuses on the negative side of human life — fetters. Due to limits in available resources, the negative evaluation of happiness is currently a theoretical hypothesis.

Even though it's argued here that the negative evaluation of happiness will better reflect the true happiness level that people experience in life, positive methods in evaluating happiness (such as subjective-well-being) do have their value. In essence, the majority of positive evaluation methods (such as HDI, GNH, or World Happiness Reports) are indicators of progress or development in areas where they are evaluated. They could be valuable tools for governments to identify problems and design and executing policies to solve these problems in societies.

How to design and conduct a negative evaluation of happiness — and how the results of this new way of measuring happiness correlate with both global happiness (life satisfaction) and domain happiness (life satisfaction) — are valuable subjects for future research and they may provide a reality-check for this novel way of measuring happiness.

CHAPTER 9:

Issues of Happiness

For anyone who has studied the current theories and research on happiness, various issues have no doubt become apparent to you regarding the implications of such research. This chapter provides examples of the issues evident in the latest research on happiness and suggests ways that the theory proposed in this book can be applied to such issues. This information will be of relevance to academic readers, particularly those who wish to tackle various issues in the field of happiness research, such as subjective well-being.

The Easterlin Paradox

The Easterlin Paradox is a key concept in happiness economics. It's named after economist and USC Professor Richard Easterlin, who discussed the factors that contribute to happiness in his 1974 paper "Does Economic Growth Improve the Human Lot? Some Empirical Evidence".[72]

In his research, he studied a data set of 30 surveys from 1946 to 1970 across 19 countries in both the developing and developed world. Easterlin observed that "within countries there is a noticeable positive association between income and happiness – in every single survey, those in the highest status group were happier, on the average, than those in the lowest status group. However, whether any such positive association exists among countries at a given time is uncertain."[72] Actually, two survey results compiled originally by Cantril, Egypt's Happiness level (5.5) is higher than West Germany (5.3) whilst West Germany had a real GDP per head (US$1860 in 1961) which is more than eight times of that of Egypt (US$225 in 1961)[92] … "Similarly, in the one national time series studied, that for the United States since 1946 (until 1970), higher income was not systematically accompanied by greater happiness."[72]

The difference between international results and those within a country has led to ongoing research into the subject. Recently, researchers have suggested that happiness *always* positively correlates with income, [93] however, this correlation is **logarithmic** rather than linear.

Close examination of the data provided by these new claims confirms the Easterlin Paradox rather than negates it. First of all, a logarithmic correlation of H (happiness) = Log X (income) denotes that at the low end of the income scale, happiness increases drastically. At the high end of the income scale, happiness barely improves with a further increase in income.

Secondly, the data shows that within a country, the correlation between an individual's happiness level and their income is significant and clearly defined.[93] However, the correlation between average happiness levels and average income between different countries is weak and vague. There are wide deviations here, particularly when incomes are above a certain level but people are still very poor.[93]

From the perspective of the happiness theory proposed in this book, the key factors in determining the happiness of an individual or group of people is fetters, which have dominant effects, not pleasures, which are momentary phenomena and more transient.

As an individual's income increases, their happiness level will increase drastically because increased income will relieve the fetters of everyday basic needs. After the basic needs of food, clothing, and shelter are met, further income increases may not raise their happiness level as quickly and apparently as before, but some financial and social fetters will improve because financial conditions do have an impact on relationships within a family.

Another important aspect of further increases in income after basic needs are met is the psychological effects on the individual. With increased income, an individual's stress at meeting the basic needs of their family and fulfilling their duties in their social life is reduced. This decrease in external stress will reduce the manifestation of mental fetters in intensity or frequency, if not eliminate them altogether.

Furthermore, the increase of an individual's income, especially if it's good compared to their peers, will make the individual feel better about themselves, whether this is motivated by gratitude or ego. A lasting benefit that an individual almost always gets from increasing their income is the improved social status attached to it, particularly in today's money-centric society.

In most cases, an increase in wealth is accompanied by success in someone's business or profession. Success in business or profession garners envy, respect, and even honour from others and society at large. This has the power to greatly reduce — if not completely eliminate — the mental fetter of inferiority. Being respected, being honoured, or even being envied by others is a pleasure in itself, but it also improves how an individual is perceived by others. This means that the social fetters felt in relationships will, in most cases, be reduced.

In money-centric societies (such as China, the U.S., and the UK), the rich and super-rich garner much envy and attention, which is pleasurable to most of them (it seems to be the only focus of Donald Trump, even after being elected to arguably the highest office in the world), as long as the fetters that are by-products of this increased income don't outpace the benefits. It's clear that in most cases, an increase in income for an individual will always increase their happiness level in an order that corresponds to Easterlin's observations about individuals.[72]

On a collective level, such as in a country where the population is very poor and basic needs are barely met, an increase in income will drastically increase the collective happiness level. With further increases in the revenue of the country, the construction of basic infrastructure such as clean water, hospitals, roads, and a social security net will relieve the majority of citizens from some physical and mental health fetters. However, contrary to individual cases, further increases in a country's average income will provide almost no benefit in psychological or social aspects. Such increases may even harm the happiness of the lower-income sections of society.

As discussed in the case of individuals, the benefits of increased income result mainly in improved psychological and social status. Collectively, when there is as much as half of the population with an above-average income, there are an equal amount of people who have a below-average income, regardless of how good the country's GDP is. So, even if a whole country is substantially better off than it was historically and/or relative to others, for every person who feels good due to their above-average income, there will be another who feels miserable because of their below-average income.

Statistically, the net benefits of increasing income as a group in psychological and social aspects are close to zero, which is exactly what the Easterlin paradox shows.[72] Worse still, when the average income level increases in a country, the perceived level of basic needs being met also increases. This is because basic needs such as food, clothing, and shelter are relative depending on both inflation and perception. The reason for this is at least two-fold.

The first is that the increase of average income normally comes with inflation, making the lives of fixed-income individuals (such as retirees) more difficult because their income isn't sufficient to meet their basic needs; inflation erodes their buying power.

The second is that the perceived level of basic needs being met is relative to the overall level of wealth that a society possesses. For example, the homeless are at the bottom of every society income-wise. However, their view of when their own basic needs are met varies depending on where they live. In many developed countries, many basic needs such as foods or clothes are met by charities for most of the year. The level of material provided would be envied not only by the homeless, but also by many average people living in ghettos in third-world countries.

However, that doesn't mean that the homeless in developed countries will feel happier than their counterparts in third world countries, such as India, because the homeless in metropolitan big cities in Europe or North America still live at the bottom of their society, compared to the affluent lives enjoyed by others surrounding them. Meagre meals, second-hand clothes, and simple over-night shelters provided by charity organisations are little to celebrate. On the contrary, statistics have shown that the homeless of Calcutta are much happier than those in Fresno, California.[33]

Why do people in unequal societies feel unhappier?

Another issue regarding happiness is the correlation between the happiness of a country and the equality of its wealth distribution. The more unequal the distribution of wealth, the less happy its population will feel on average,[94] although according to the most recent World

Happiness Report, other factors such as social or cultural issues may play a more important role in people's perception of happiness than income. [67]

Using the happiness theory proposed in this book, the negative impact of unevenly allocated national wealth on the average level of happiness can be explained as follows: after basic needs are met (and these fetters are eliminated), the main benefits that more income provides are social and psychological ones, all of which are relative to other people.

When wealth distribution is very unequal with a few super-rich individuals and a poor majority, there are many people struggling around the poverty line who barely meet their basic needs, whilst the extra wealth of the super-rich brings them almost no extra happiness.

Furthermore, there are more people to feel worse off than there are people to feel better off. Statistically, the average level of happiness in a country will be lower than the average level of a country with a similar average income but with a more equal wealth distribution (provided that other social and cultural conditions are similar).

If the wealth of the minority is accumulated by unfair means such as corruption, then the average happiness level will be even worse. This is because the benefits of increased income for the rich and successful would be overtaken by hatred from their fellow citizens. This may be why Russia and other former Soviet countries have experienced such low levels of happiness since the move from communism to a market-oriented economy, where a few oligarchies became extremely rich through their closeness to power whilst the majority fell into poverty. Considering their average income, their average happiness is among the worst in the world.

The paradox of hedonism

First explicitly noted by Henry Sidgwick in *The Methods of Ethics*, the paradox of hedonism points out that "pleasure cannot be acquired directly, it can only be acquired indirectly." [95] In other words, the more deliberately you seek out pleasure, the less likely you are to actually find it.

As discussed, pleasures are nothing but a temporary shield against fetters. When we make pleasure our direct target, doing things for the sake of pleasure rather than for the thing itself, then we ask ourselves questions like "am I having fun yet?" As soon as such questions are asked consciously, our attention will automatically focus on the self, which is full of fetters.

As soon as our attention is focused on ourselves, the pleasure goes. This is why people with big egos or who are self-centred are more likely to be unhappy than those who have similar life conditions but are less self-centred. One of the main reasons why film stars and pop stars seldom live happy lives is because of their egocentric personality. Meanwhile, those who are busy helping others, such as volunteers in all kinds of social and community services, are found to be among the happiest in society.[33]

When we involve and occupy ourselves in volunteer work, we simply forget our own problems and quite often enter a condition similar to Flow (if not as intense). When we encounter others less fortunate than ourselves, the problems we have in our daily life don't seem so overwhelming. We're more likely to be content or even grateful for what we have and less likely to complain about what we don't have. In such situations, we're not unhappy.

What's more, when we see the results of our efforts, perhaps with a genuine smile and a "thank you" from someone, we feel love towards the people we've helped. When love or compassion occupies our mind, negative emotions or chaotic thoughts cannot take centre stage in our consciousness. This is one of the reasons why good things happen to good people.[96]

The hedonic treadmill and set-point theory

The hedonic treadmill,[97] also known as hedonic adaption, means human beings' apparent tendency to return to a relatively stable level of happiness *relatively* quickly after any significant positive or negative events or changes in their life, such as losing a loved one or gaining a promotion. In the latter example, although the individual makes more money, their desires and expectations also increase, and so their increased income does not result in a long-term improvement in their happiness levels. They merely go back to what they were before the promotion.

This idea underpins the set-point theory of happiness, which suggests that each individual has a fixed level of average happiness i.e. our set point. Around this point, our level of happiness each day in every moment may vary, but we will quickly return to our set point after a significant event. Research by Brickman et all (1978) [98]supported this, finding that lottery winners were not significantly happier than those with spinal cord injuries after their initial excitement at winning wore off. Unfortunately, this theory suggests that we will never get any happier with means we have in our lives.

Similarly, the research's results suggest that adult subjective well-being (or happiness) is relatively stable over the medium and long term, although temporary fluctuations occur due to life events.[97,57,99] However, there have been numerous research studies challenging the implications of set-point theory based on a wide range of evidence.[100,101,10,102,103]

Large-scale panel data from three countries over a period up to 25 years showed that life choices such as life goals/values, partner's personality, hours of work and leisure, social participation, and healthy lifestyles have substantial effects on life satisfaction.[104]

Moreover, persistent change is fairly significant in up to a third of any population[100] and persistent and repeated unemployment has been shown to have a long-term effect on subjective well-being.[101] Health, particularly chronic conditions, and family are domains in which long-term change is quite likely to occur.[10] For example, late-onset health problems such as type two diabetes and arthritis permanently lower subjective well-being.[102,103]

With so much evidence at odds with set-point theory, some economists have declared that it is simply wrong.[10;11] The arguments against it are not about the stability of subjective well-being for the majority of people[100] or the dominant effect of genetics on a person's subjective well-being, but about the sweeping inference that a person's subjective well-being is a stochastic (randomly determined) phenomenon,[57] not based on any life events or personal choices.

As opponents of set-point theory (mainly utility-focused economists) admit, the majority of people have a relatively stable level of subjective well-being for 25 years.[100] Statistical research has also found that around only one-seventh of individual variance in subjective well-being is accounted for by the combination of financial situation, family life, health, and work.[51]

As argued throughout this book, the dominant factors affecting an individual's happiness or subjective well-being are internal fetters, particularly negative emotions, chaotic thoughts, and excessive desires. Other than in extreme events such as war (which may lead to post-traumatic stress disorder), internal fetters are usually very stable throughout adult life. I believe that this set of stable traits (such as levels of negative emotions, chaotic thoughts, and desires in an individual) underline the fact that the majority of people maintain a stable level of subjective well-being over decades.[100,51]

Although internal fetters such as negative emotions, chaotic thoughts, and desires play an extremely important role in the happiness of an individual, they aren't the only fetters that affect a person's subjective well-being in the short or long term. Physical health fetters, basic fetters, environmental fetters, and social fetters also have an effect. Most people are subjected to the influence of the micro and macro environments we live in, and these will change over time. When they change significantly over a period of time, an individual or group of people's subjective well-being level will change as a result. When this happens, strict set-point theory will fail to explain the reality of life, as it doesn't count all the factors that play a part in a person or group's subjective well-being, for example, health issues such as developing a degenerative condition or losing a job.

As pointed out by Easterlin,[10] hedonic adaption does happen in the financial domain. The key to happiness (life satisfaction) is fewer fetters rather than more money.[51] Financial satisfaction results more from financial freedom than from the extra utilities that money can buy us, as has traditionally been believed by economists. Financial freedom is one of the main benefits of being rich, but it doesn't solely depend on your annual income or net worth, nor is it determined by your financial position in relation to others. Financial freedom is the point at which your life is no longer significantly negatively affected by money issues.

Case study: the graduate student with a tight budget

As a graduate student, I had a young family of three. My meagre research assistantship was our main income. We carefully budgeted so we could get by and not get too deep into debt. However, when we visited new and unfamiliar places, particularly expensive cities like New York, I always got anxious when we were looking for a restaurant to eat in. It was an embarrassment, even in front of our 6-year-old boy, to say we had to find another restaurant because we couldn't afford that one, even though we were all hungry. Years later when our financial conditions were greatly improved, one of my greatest satisfactions was the ability to walk into an unfamiliar restaurant that looked expensive and luxurious without worrying about the cost. It's not that we dine in plush restaurants more often nowadays that gives me satisfaction (we actually dine out far less than we used to); it's the fact that theoretically we can afford to.

Financial freedom depends on our financial resources and obligations. Retired people who earn much less are happier financially than during their prime working years when they earned significantly more.[51] During the late part of adult life, financial obligations such as mortgages and car loans have been paid off, meaning that major financial fetters are finally unloaded. A few delights in life (dream holidays, flash cars, etc.) are easily met with our financial resources. Even with less income in retirement, we feel happier financially because we have fewer obligations or fetters than during our prime years. Thus, the financial satisfaction or freedom shown in long-term surveys is higher during retirement than during our working years.[51]

However, hedonic adaption does not happen in all cases, even with material possessions. The hedonic treadmill implies that you have to change (keep on earning more) to maintain the same level of happiness. If you do the same old thing again and again, you won't have fun anymore.

Yet, people who collect classic cars for a hobby do so for years without any loss of pleasure in spending time restoring and appreciating them, even if the cars seem like junk to others. There is a difference between them and people who simply own a car as a means of transport or for social status. To the vast majority of car owners, the novelty of a new car will soon wane and therefore, so will the owner's interest in the car itself. People quickly almost stop noticing their car until there's a problem with it. So, the key to continuous pleasure through ownership of an object is found in continuous interest in the object itself.

For most people in today's mainstream consumer society, keeping up with fashion is the main motivation for buying and possessing consumer goods. The interest is not in the goods themselves but in their ability to bring a sense of self-esteem, a sense of being up to date. As soon as a new, "better", more fashionable version of a product comes on the market, the old product loses its appeal, perhaps even becoming a burden if the person has to use it because they can't afford the new version.

Other than material possessions, exceptions to the hedonic treadmill happen in other aspects of life as well. Flow experiences are excellent examples of exceptions to hedonic adaption. Different people experience Flow in different activities, but people rarely change their favourite Flow activities throughout their life. Instead, many people maintain their hobbies for a lifetime. People who love skiing will keep on skiing into their senior years, just as people who love dancing, golfing, chess, fishing, or music will continue their passion. People not only enjoy their hobbies with unhampered enthusiasm, but they can also enjoy the same activities in exactly the same location over many years. The home-river or home-water for an angler is as cosy, as comfortable, as life ever could offer.

As long as people have deep interest or affection in an activity, doing that activity will continue to bring them fun and pleasure no matter how long they've been doing it or how many times they've done it. People will never tire of doing their Flow activities, even if they seem repetitive and boring in other people's eyes. As long as they still have a deep interest, that's all that counts.

Exceptions to the hedonic treadmill can also be found in human relationships. As an adult, we maintain pretty much the same friendships and social circles as long as we don't change our workplace. We keep the same group of old friends who we share jokes with. It's rare for ordinary people to enjoy meeting a new person. It's often uncomfortable and can cause anxiety — ask someone how they feel when they're going to meet their future in-laws for the first time!

Obviously, it's not always the case that change causes pleasure, as claimed by some psychologists.[105] We enjoy the company of old friends for as long as we're interested in the same topics of conversation or enjoy the same activities as them. However, old friends become alienated when parted for a long period of time. When we meet our best friends from childhood, we won't feel as much pleasure as we did in the first few moments of the joyful reunion. The reason is because we no longer share the same interests, and more often than not, we don't share the same values either. Without the resonation of our personal interests and mutual approval of our values and judgments, the fun or pleasure of the relationship with our childhood friends will be no more than a fond memory.

As we've seen, the hedonic treadmill suggests that after a major disaster or tragedy, people will eventually return to their normal level of happiness. But this is only true when the major disaster or tragedy doesn't result in persistent and lasting new fetters. For example, people who have lost limbs or been paralysed after an accident often return to the same level of happiness they had before the accident.[35] However, if pain or suffering continues to be present, then people are generally not able to adapt. For example, paraplegics often adapt to new limits without a significant loss of happiness in their lives,[35] while chronic illness sufferers are rarely able to get used to their illnesses.[102,103]

We don't hear of chronic insomniacs adapting to insomnia, even if they've suffered with it for years, just as we don't see chronic depression sufferers adapting to the pain of depression. The reason is that for a paraplegic, the tragedy caused pain at the time of the accident and during their recovery, but when the physical pain stops, many people come to accept their new reality of limited physical movement.

Without physical pains and with the acceptance of a new lifestyle, there aren't many extra fetters for a paraplegic, particularly if they experience understanding and assistance from society at large. However, for a chronic insomniac or someone suffering from prolonged depression, the pain and sadness form an everyday reality, which is constantly sensed and felt by them. The fetter causing pain and suffering is still there, so the sufferer will never be able to adapt completely. Many chronic diseases and conditions have similar effects, such as migraine, hay fever, eczema, arthritis, and other mental disorders. If physical or mental pain is continuously present, then people will generally not be able to adapt.

In the realm of relationships, the closer and stronger the inter-personal relationships, the more they will affect us, both positively and negatively, as discussed in chapter five. People who lose close family members will be affected similarly. Most people will feel sad when they face the tragedy of unexpected loss such as the death of a baby, child, or any other sudden and premature death. Yet how people react during the period after the tragedy determines whether their life and overall level of happiness will be compromised or not.

If they accept the loss and proceed with other aspirations or interests that occupy their life fully (particularly when the goal of those interests is higher than an individual goal), then the tragedy may be a little easier to accept; its effects becoming less harrowing over time. Eventually, the impact on their level of happiness will be minimal. However, if the person cannot accept the loss and always dwells on memories of the loved one, particularly where there are also deep negative feelings of regret, guilt, or sorrow, then the loss will continue to affect their happiness in a major way.[106]

In summary, for the majority of people, their subjective well-being is relatively stable during their adult lives[100,55] and the stability of their subjective well-being results mainly from internal conditions and individual personality, particularly the part related to mental fetters, chaotic thoughts, and desires.

Hedonic adaption occurs when people lose interest in objects or activities. However, if interest still exists, then hedonic adaption will not happen, such as when people enjoy their Flow activities throughout a lifetime. When negative events happen, hedonic adaption occurs if there are no new long-lasting fetters created by the event, allowing people to return to their previous level of happiness. However, if the event creates persistent and long-lasting new fetters, then the well-being of the person will be affected in the long term and adaption will not happen.

CHAPTER 10:

Who Are the Happiest People on Earth?

Let's consider who the happiest people are. Is it the fabulously rich? The most famous celebrities? Royalty? Political heavyweights? Perhaps, if Ancient Greek wisdom remains true, it's philosophers?[5] In this chapter, we'll look at who the happiest people truly are.

The rich and famous

The rich and famous have been envied since humans first started to realise differences among themselves. They were the ones we regarded as fortunate, role models we wanted to emulate or people that our kids looked up to. They seem to not only occupy the centre-stage of society but they naturally seem to come to mind when we wonder who the happiest people in the world are. In an age where religious and traditional values exert an ever-smaller influence, these people are the idols that some go as far as to worship.

As glamorous and glorious as they are in the eyes of others, the rich and famous have many fetters that most people aren't aware of. As we saw in chapter seven, money can relieve the rich of fetters such as food, clothing, shelter, and financial worries.

However, the rich and famous, no matter how much insurance they can buy, are still as helpless as everyone else when it comes to illnesses such as cancer, heart attacks, and diabetes. They have to suffer the terrible pain accompanying these illnesses just like everyone else. Steve Jobs might have been the king of technology during the latter part of his life, and his wealth could be compared with that of a small nation, but it didn't prevent him becoming a victim of pancreatic cancer. He had to suffer the brutal pains of that illness for years.[107] The rich and famous aren't immune to natural disasters and flukes either.

It may surprise "ordinary" people that celebrities have to pay an extra price for their wealth and celebrity status, which is losing the freedom to live a normal life. They lose the freedom of basic things as simple as a quiet, casual stroll in public areas. For example, singer Taylor Swift recently lamented her difficulty in dating and striking up normal relationships.[108] With the paparazzi and the public following celebrities everywhere and intruding into every part of their lives, a task as mundane as driving their children to school can become a nightmare. Celebrities often resort to isolating themselves, as the freedom of living a normal life is the price they have to pay for their success. They become public pets: adorable in the eyes of onlookers but living in a cage nevertheless.

The loss of freedom isn't all either. The rich and famous often have far more troubles and worries because they have to take care of more matters than an ordinary person does. They may suffer from more mental fetters or even mental illnesses than others. The intensity of their mental fetters seems stronger, and their mental illnesses seem more insidious, as the high rate of substance abuse among them shows (we'll look at this in more depth in the next book).[109] Some celebrities die young, with the so-called "27 Club" providing anecdotal evidence of what can become of superstars in the music and movie industries.[109]

Those who are rich but not fabulously famous might be able to avoid some of the pitfalls mentioned here, but they still have to bear most of the same fetters as ordinary people. Sometimes, wealth itself can become a burden. The wealthy have one more thing to worry about than us: losing their money! Redundant wealth, the wealth or assets that people possess but will never need or use (other than as an inheritance to bequeath when they die), can become a true fetter to them.

Such wealth, often invested in stocks or other business assets, is subject to the ups and downs of markets and business cycles. Like anyone else, those who have redundant wealth have the worry of losing it when the stock market or economy is in a downturn, but they could lose tons of money simply because they own so much in the first place — and this becomes particularly clear in an economic crisis.

There is little joy to be found when the economy is strong either, since so much is already owned and any gains are nothing but a number in an investment account. Compared to someone who owns no stock, those who are heavily invested in the stock market have to bear the worries and stresses of losing it, particularly during a financial crash. Owning assets other than stocks and bonds is also subject to loss if not cared for properly. Caring for anything means trouble and burdens for the person who owns it.

Losing money is not the only thing that the rich have to worry about. They have all the troubles and worries of owning a business. They have to worry about others stealing or taking advantage of their wealth. In fact, the latter often taints their relationships with those close to them. These people may have more difficulty forming true and genuine friendships — partly because they're more alert and suspicious of the intentions of others, and partly because others may not want a close relationship with them due to jealousy or lack of things in common. Sometimes, money can even turn family members into sworn enemies. Thus, the super-rich regularly end up living a life lonelier than ordinary people, lacking the happiness of engagement with others.

The glamour of the rich and famous also deceives many "ordinary" people who fix their hopes of happiness on marrying a rich, famous man or woman, or one who has the potential to become successful, rich, and famous. The delusion often bursts not long after the honeymoon or a few years into their marriage. To be extremely successful in any area requires people to devote all of their time and energy into their work. This leaves them with little time and energy for their partner and children when they come back home at night. It's almost a given that the partner of a rich and famous person has to give up their own ambitions to take care of their partner and children.

But the bitterest pill for such people to swallow is the feeling of being neglected, not cherished by the person of their affection. They feel they deserve attention for the sacrifice they have made. The mansion and other luxuries they envied and longed for before marriage become a prison where they wait, lonely, for their partner's return. The rich, famous person thinks they have already fulfilled their responsibilities by providing luxuries for their family. Having worked long, hectic hours, they feel they deserve extra care and warmth from the non-famous partner who has been at home doing "nothing". Sooner or later, a clash of emotions is inevitable and the marriage will end up in a precarious condition.

The only gain that the rich and famous may derive from their wealth, particularly redundant wealth, is the satisfaction of their ego. The satisfaction of ego and desires are at best a fleeting moment of pleasure in life and (as we saw in the discussion on desires) are nothing but fetters to us. Thus, the rich and famous may be a little happier than ordinary people,[10] but they still have many of the same fetters as ordinary people, plus some extra ones that come with wealth and fame. They are arguably not the happiest people in the world.

The powerful

The powerful, the kings and queens of the past and the political heavyweights of today, don't fare much better than the rich and famous in the happiness arena. Most of them may be rich and famous too, meaning they have the same fetters to deal with. Also, people in power are forever entangled in power struggles. They may live in constant fear and have to be alert to all kinds of dangers and worries because in politics, there are no friends — only temporary allies. Everybody else is a potential enemy.

They not only have to worry about the big issues of state but also their own political career, personal safety, and the safety of their families. Even the luckiest among them, powerful public figures in modern democracies without much worry of politically-motivated assassination, are still potential targets for terrorist attacks or disturbed individuals. U.S. president Ronald Reagan being shot by John Hinckley in 1981 is a perfect example of the latter. They're the prisoners of stricter incarceration than the rich and famous as they have less freedom to live a normal life, both physically and mentally.

Entrepreneurs and skilled professionals

It may surprise many people that some successful entrepreneurs, such as small- and medium-sized business owners and well-accomplished professionals, live the happiest life in an ordinary sense. Small- and medium-sized business owners not only reap the benefits of financial success but perhaps, more importantly, enjoy the independence of being their own boss.

Successful professionals who love what they do and are happy with their status, whether a renowned scientist or a well-respected IT technician, are the people exploiting and enjoying their full potential in today's society. They enjoy success in their line of work and earn enough money to live a comfortable, if not particularly luxurious, life. More importantly, they enjoy genuine respect from their peers and the people around them. Just as importantly, these people truly enjoy their jobs and are good at them. They reap all the benefits of being successful: confidence, self-esteem, freedom, autonomy where applicable, full engagement in their work, and enjoying their time with other people in their professions and daily life.

Unlike high-level politicians or CEOs who are forever "putting out fires", small- and medium-sized business owners, due to their comparatively anonymous status, don't have all the fetters that come with recognition and large organisations. The limited scale of their businesses and professions offer far less stress than the rich and famous suffer, allowing them to enjoy more of their work and the challenges it offers.

But is that all it is? Is that the best life we can achieve? How can well-known scientists and competent professionals live the best life a human can hope for? We all know someone in such categories who proves the opposite: the highly respected professor at a prestigious university whose meanness is legendary, the well-liked IT technician with a drinking problem, and so on. Such examples are too commonplace for us to rate these people as the happiest in the world.

The problem with such notions

The problem with this notion — that such people could be the happiest — is that it only points to those who have the best *conditions* for happiness, but isn't a guarantee of it. The biggest challenges facing mankind, however good their external conditions, are **internal**. Even with an ideal external life — material wealth, career success, a loving and caring family, a supportive and friendly working environment, and living in a peaceful, humane, harmonious, democratic free society — people can still suffer from strong internal fetters such as depression. Three insurmountable mountains block ordinary people's path to the promised land of the long-lasting happiness: negative emotions, a chaotic mindset, and excessive desires.

With determination and hard work, wealth, power, and fame are achievable. With luck, health and beauty are also possible, but long-lasting happiness is out of reach for the vast majority of ordinary people. The three mountains prevent us from reaching happiness, no matter who we are or how well we do in life.

The sages

Are we truly doomed in our pursuit of long-lasting happiness, then? Throughout history, great philosophers such as Aristotle, St Augustine, Aquinas, Locke, and Rousseau have lamented that happiness will forever elude us and that only the hope we have is for a happy life in heaven.[5]

But is true, long-lasting happiness on earth possible? After two millennia of philosophical deliberation by the greatest human minds to the contrary, the cries and longing for that ultimate prize in life are as clear today as at any time in history. Thankfully, the answer is yes!

It's arguable that the happiest humans who ever lived and are living on earth are the sages. These are the "realised" people, high-level yogis, living "Buddhas" (in quotation marks as some Buddhists don't believe there is a living Buddha in the world today), accomplished Qi Gong masters, and so on. People may be surprised to learn this.

Ironically, these are the people who are least interested in the things we normally associate with happiness, such as wealth, fame, and power. As people seeking happiness in the delusions of money and success, we're similarly misled in trying to find the happiest people by looking in those areas.

As the central theme of this book states, happiness is the freedom from fetters — and all that pleasures bring us is temporary relief or freedom from our fetters. It follows then that the happiest people aren't those with the most material wealth, fame, or power in life, but those with the fewest fetters. It's ironic that we pursue happiness by trying to get "more" – more money, more power, more fame, more this and more that, when real happiness lies in having "less": less pain, less stress, less worry, less troubles, and less fetters.

Sages are the very few human beings (referred to as "abnormal" in chapter four) who have been truly free from most of the fetters described here, particularly the internal ones. They are the "true-man" and "ultra-man", as described in *The Yellow Emperor's Classic of Internal Medicine*[110], who breach the boundary between human and divinity, constantly living their lives in harmony with Tao (the divine).

We know relatively little about sages save the superior wisdom they possess in comparison to ordinary people. However, a distinctive and well-known characteristic of sages is that they have surmounted the three insurmountable mountains of ordinary human beings: negative emotions, chaotic minds, and excessive desires. They conquered these mountains, achieving a pure heart and mind with unlimited brightness. What Plato prescribed for his philosopher kings, "the one who, living in constant companionship with the divine order of the world, will reproduce that order in his soul, and so far as man may, becoming godlike"[20], has (almost) reached these pinnacles.

Schopenhauer[16] vividly described the mental life of those who've achieved sage-like inner status when he wrote "blessed must be the life of a man whose will is silenced not for a few moments, as in the enjoyment of the beautiful, but forever, indeed completely extinguished, except for the last glimmering spark that maintains the body and is extinguished with it. Such a man who, after many bitter struggles with his own nature, has at last completely conquered, is then left only as pure knowing being, as the undimmed mirror of the world. Nothing can distress or alarm him anymore; nothing can any longer move him; for he has cut all the thousand threads of willing which hold us bound to the world, and which as craving, fear, envy, and anger drag us here and there in constant pain. He now looks back calmly and with a smile on the phantasmagoria of this world which was once able to move and agonize his mind, but now stands before him as indifferently as chess-men at the end of a game, or as fancy dress cast off in the morning, the form and figure of which taunted and disquieted us on the carnival night. Life and its forms merely float before him as a fleeting phenomenon, as a light morning dream to one half-awake, through which reality already shines, and which can no longer deceive; and, like this morning dream, they too finally vanish without any violent transition."[16]

Hinduism offers a similar description in *Yoga Vasistha*, a spiritual text of the Advaita school, which states: "Pleasures do not delight him; pains do not distress. Although engaged in worldly actions, he has no attachment to any object. He is busy outwardly yet calm inwardly. He feels free from restrictions of scriptures, customs, age, caste or creed. He is happy, but his happiness does not depend on anything else. He does not feel needy, proud, agitated, troubled, depressed or elated. He is full of compassion and forgiveness even to those who mean him harm. He does the right thing, regardless of the pressures. He is patient, perseverant, and without any impurity in his heart. He is free of delusions; he does not crave for anything. His sense of freedom comes from his spirit of inquiry. The fruits of his inquiry are his strength, intellect, efficiency and punctuality. He keeps the company of wise and enlightened persons. He is content."

Sages are not even chained by basic fetters as some of them can live without eating food (known as "bigu", an ancient oriental technique of obtaining immortality of the physical body and a way of obtaining energy through meditation). Some can even control their body temperature and environment.[111] Most importantly, they have settled their heart and minds, enabling them to reach a status of unlimited brightness.

Do not judge sages by their looks, their outfits, or (lack of) fame. A sage could be a beggar (seemingly their preferred guise in legends), a peasant, or anything similar. They're not necessarily dressed in impressive robes or well-known to others because they seek anonymity over fame.

Sages aren't without feelings; they're full of compassion for ordinary people who suffer from all kinds of pain, even though they are personally liberated from such suffering. They will do everything in their power to alleviate pain and suffering for others, without the slightest arrogance so often displayed by many of the rich and powerful in the world. Their dignity humbles us; it seems boundless in their hearts and they are all-pervading in their love and compassion. They genuinely forgive those who seem unforgivable to us. More often than not, we come upon them when they live among us as very ordinary people with unmistakable charisma.

However, sages may choose a hermetic life when society is in the middle of collective madness and there is very little they can do to alleviate suffering. They have a clear picture and understanding of the plagues and problems of ordinary people in society. Yet instead of being sarcastic or cynical about such problems, they are full of compassion for the unprivileged and those who are suffering. They are not angered, overwhelmed, or disturbed by outer madness and can deal with any crisis in front of them with unshakeable equanimity.

Even Nietzsche, who worshipped the ego, the will to power of his "superman", had to admit there were things that even the lion (the apex of power) could not do, and that the lion must transform himself to the pure child beyond.[5]

Many will probably not believe that the sages described here truly exist in the world today. They will claim that stories about sages are nothing but legends, that what is described here is pure imagination or wishful thinking. However, modern science can provide at least some evidence that may give us a glimpse of the happiest person on earth.[112] Matthieu Ricard, a French biologist turned Tibetan monk, scored the highest out of everyone examined by happiness researchers at the University of Wisconsin-Madison. Dr Ricard admitted that he has not yet reached sage status but seemed to be on his way there, as confirmed in his books and interviews.[113] However, he has already been declared the happiest person alive, at least out of those who were tested. Imagine how happy he would be if he reached true sage-hood.

CONCLUSION:

Finding Happiness

Since ancient times, people have been seeking happiness. It seems that everybody knows when they are happy or not, whilst even the wisest don't know what exactly happiness is.

The Ancient Greek philosophers regarded happiness highly, as Socrates stated that happiness is human's ultimate desire and Aristotle claimed that happiness is the highest good (Telos) for humans. Traditional Christians' understanding of happiness is forever beatitude in heaven when this life on earth is over. The Buddhists' also believe that life on earth is suffering. On the other hand, modern day philosophers (and economists and psychologists) are more acceptive of a hedonic understanding of happiness as pleasure, though with some reluctance.

This book argues that happiness is experienced via our faculty of awareness. We have four to five levels of awareness, namely bodily awareness, mental awareness, thought awareness, ethical awareness, and even spiritual awareness. We experience every moment of life through a dynamic equilibrium of both positive and negative experiences in all four to five levels of awareness, in a similar way to a tribunal.

The negative side of that dynamic equilibrium is fetters, whilst the positive side is positive experiences in both our relationships and activities. Most previous understandings of happiness focus on only the positive side, whereas the happiness theory proposed in this book emphasizes the importance of the negative side of the dynamic equilibrium of human experiences. It argued that fetters have more of an influence on human happiness than the positive sides of experiences such as pleasures.

We have both external fetters, which may be affected by external factors, and internal fetters, which are barely affected by outside factors. External fetters include basic bodily fetters such as hunger, thirst, coldness, financial fetters, environmental fetters, and social fetters. Internal fetters include illnesses, mental fetters, and excessive desires. Due to the omnipresence of internal fetters (particularly negative emotions, chaotic thoughts, and excessive desires), internal fetters play a decisive role in determining our overall level of happiness.

Positive experiences such as pleasure in both relationships and activities provide us with temporary relief (freedom) from the shackles of fetters. Positive relationships with others are basic ingredients of happiness in life for most people. Lack of them is the cause of loneliness. In particular, Flow[13] is the optimum human life experience where people enjoy the process itself in addition to the goal. However, Flow experiences total only a very small fraction of most people's lives. Sub-Flow activities play a more important role in most people's daily lives. In sub-Flow processes, the goal is the main or only focus. Most important life processes such as school learning and jobs are mainly sub-Flow processes where goals are the focal points.

Generally, our pleasures and gratifications from childhood lead us to believe that we will be happy if we could become a millionaire or become someone (successful), which are the delusions of money and success. Most people live their entire life pursuing these delusions without realizing they are chasing the wind. However, when people truly reach success, they might encounter a mid-life crisis when their delusional bubble of success burst as they have lost their goals. Thus, they experience a catastrophic lack of happiness.

As fetters play a more important role in determining how happy we are in life than positive experiences such as pleasures, it is proposed here that we should calculate happiness using fetters more than the elusive feeling of "good" in other methods, such as utilitarianism or subjective well-being. The theory proposed here explains some outstanding paradoxes and phenomena in happiness research. It also provides a reality check for the theory's validity in real life.

In the end, what a joke life has played with us humans! We have been pursuing happiness since time immemorial by trying to have all of the "good things" in life, such as wealth, fame, and power. Ultimately, however, it's the "have not", the lack of fetters, that is the magic key to true, long-lasting happiness. Something that only sages seem able to achieve.

The double irony is that sages not only exist in today's world, but theoretically-speaking, sage-hood is within reach for all of us! How can we obtain true long-lasting happiness, perhaps even sage-hood, and why we should want to do so are some of the main subjects covered in the next book of this series: *How to Obtain Happiness and Why*.

REFERENCES

1. Plato. *Early Socratic Dialogues.* Saunders, Trevor J. 1987. New York: Penguin Books.

2. Aristotle, *Nichomachean Ethics.* 2004. London: Penguin books.

3. James, William. 1994, *The Varieties of Religious Experiences.* New York: Modern Library.

4. Wilson, Eric G. 2008. *Against Happiness.* New York: Farrar, Straus and Giroux.

5. McMahon, Darrin M. 2006. *HAPPINESS, A HISTORY.* New York: Grove Press.

6. Cheng, Sheung-Tak. 1988. "SUBJECTIVE QUALITY OF LIFE IN THE PLANNING AND EVALUATION OF PROGRAMS." *Evaluation and Program Planning*, Vol 11, PP. 123-134.

7. Deng, Ming-Dao. 1993. *Chronicles of Tao.* New York: Harper Collins Publishers.

8. Wilson W. 1967. "Correlates of avowed happiness." *Psychological Bulletin*, 67, 294-306.

9. Diener E., Suh E. M., Lucas R. E., Smith H. L. 1999. "Subjective Well-Being: Three Decades of Progress." *Psychological Bulletin*, Vol. 125, No. 2, 276-302.

10. Easterlin, R. A. 2005. "Building a better theory of well-being." In L. Bruni & P. Porta (Eds.), *Economics and happiness: Framing the analysis.* Oxford University Press.

11. Layard Richard. 2011. *HAPPINESS LESSONS FROM A NEW SCIENCE.* London: Penguin Books.

12. Epicurus. 1993. *The Essential Epicurus-letters, principal doctrines, Vatican sayings and fragments.* Buffalo, NY: Prometheus Books.

13. Csikszentmihalyi, Mihaly. 1990. *Flow.* New York: Harper Collins Publishers.

14. Epictetus (Translated and with an introduction by A. A. Long). 2018. *How to be free.* Princeton, NJ: Princeton University Press.

15. Aurelius Marcus. 2011. *The Meditations.* London: Collector's Library.

16. Schopenhauer, Arthur. *THE WORLD AS WILL AND REPRESENTATION.* (translated from German by E.F.J, Payne). 1969. New York: Dover Publications.

17. Sheehy, Gail. 2006. *PASSAGES.* New York: Ballantine Books.

18. STIGLITZ, Joseph E. et al. 2009. *SURVEY OF EXISTING APPROACHES TO MEASURING SOCIO-ECONOMIC PROGRESS.* Commission on the Measurement of Economic Performance and Social Progress.

19. Martin Mike W. 2012. *Happiness and the Good Life.* New York: Oxford University Press.

20. Plato, *THE REPUBLIC.* 2,000. New York: Dover Publications.

21. Seneca. *Moral Essays*, (trans. John Basore, 3 vols. Cambridge, Mass.: Harvard University Press. 1992).

22. Augustine, *The Happy Life.* (trans. Ludwig Schopp.1948 New York: Cima Publishing.)

23. Aquinas, *Summa contra Gentiles, book 3*, (trans. P Sigmund. 1988. New York: W. W. Norton.)

24. Calvin, John. *The Institute of the Christian Religion*, (trans. Allen, John. 1949. 8th ed. 2 vols. Grand Rapids, Mich.: William B. Eerdmans Publishing Company).

25. Boethius. *The Consolation of Philosophy.* (Watts, V. E. 1998. London, UK: Folio Society.)

26. ATTAR, Farid Ud-Din (translated by Afkham Darbandi and Dick Davis). 1984. *The Conference of the Birds.* New York: Penguin Books.

27. Feuerstein, Georg. 1996. *The Philosophy of Classical Yoga.* Rochester Vermont: Inner Traditions International.

28. Locke, John. *An Essay concerning Human Understanding.* 1975. New York: Oxford University Press.

29. Rousseau, J. J. *Reveries of the Solitary Walker.* (trans. Goulbourne Russell. 2011. Oxford: Oxford University Press.)

30. Hobbes, Thomas. *Leviathan.* 2006. Mineola, NY: Dover Publications.

31. Ryan Alan. *John Stuart Mill and Jeremy Bentham – Utilitarianism and Other Essays*. 1987. London: Penguin Books.

32. Ricard, Matthieu. 2003. *Happiness A GUIDE TO DEVELOPING LIFE'S MOST IMPORTANT SKILL*. New York: Little, Brown and Company.

33. Seligman, Martin E. P. 2003, *AUTHENTIC HAPPINESS*. Boston: Nicholas Brealey Publishing.

34. Seligman, Martin E. P. 2011. *Flourish*. New York: Free Press.

35. Wortman, Camille B. & Silver, Roxane C. 1989. "The Myths of Coping with Loss." *J. of Consulting and Clinical Psychology*, Vol. 57, No. 3, 349-357.

36. Cohen Philip N. "The coming divorce decline". *Family Inequality*, September, 2018.

37. Myers David and Diener Ed. 1995. "WHO IS HAPPY?" *Psychological Science*, Volume 6, No.1 Jan., 1995, Page 10 – 17.

38. Klein, Stefan. 2015. *THE SCIENCE OF HAPPINESS*. Scribe UK: Da Capo Lifelong Books.

39. Chalmers, David. 1997. *The Conscious Mind: In Search of a Fundamental Theory*. Oxford: Oxford University Press.

40. Haidt, Jonathan. 2006. *The Happiness Hypothesis, Finding Modern Truth in Ancient Wisdom*. New York: Basic Books.

41. Kant, Immanuel (translated by Lewis White Beck). 1989. *Fundamental principles of the metaphysics of ethics*. London: Macmillan Publishing Company.

42. Hume, David. 1826. *AN ENQUIRY CONCERNING THE PRINCIPLES OF MORALS* from The Philosophical Works of David Hume, vol. 4, Edinburgh.

43. Maslow, A. 1954. *Motivation and personality*. New York: Harper.

44. Berlin, Isaiah. 2004. *Liberty, Five Essays on Liberty: An Introduction*, page 33-4. Oxford. (requoted from Wikipedia).

45. American Psychiatric Association. 2013. *DSM – 5: Diagnostic and Statistical Manual of Mental Disorders, 5th Edition*.

46. Chaney Sarah, Ph. D. 2013. *Self-Mutilation and Psychiatry: Impulse, Identity and the Unconscious in British Explanations of Self-Inflicted Injury, c. 1864 – 1914*. Thesis, History of Medicine, University College London.

47. Kant, I. (translated by Humphrey, T.) 1983. *Perpetual Peace and Other Essays*. Indianapolis: Hackett Classics.

48. Mill, J. S. 2006. *On Liberty*. Minneapolis: FILIQUARIAN PUBLISHING LLC

49. Epictetus (translated by Long, A.A.) 2018. How to Be Free – An Ancient Guide to the Stoic Life. Princeton: Princeton University Press

50. Krishnamurti.1996. *Total Freedom: The Essential Krishnamurti*. San Francisco: HarperOne

51. Easterlin, R. A. 2005. "Is There an 'Iron Law of Happiness'." *IEPR WORKING PAPER 05.8*. Institute of Economic Policy Research, University of Southern California.

52. John Hopkin's University of Medicine, Coronavirus Resource Center. July 30, 2020.Baltimore, Maryland.

53. Bureau of Labor Statistics, US Department of Labor. July 2, 2020. *News Release*. USDL-20-1310

54. Headey, B; Muffels, Ruud J. A., & Wagner, G. 2013. "Choices which change life satisfaction: Similar results for Australia, Britain and Germany." *Social Indicators Research*, 112(3), 725-748.

55. Benedict, Ruth. 1989. *THE CHRYSANTHEMUM AND THE SWORD*. Boston: Houghton Mifflin Company.

56. Lykken, D., & Tellegen, A. 1996. "Happiness is a stochastic phenomenon." *Psychological Science, 7*, 186-189.

57. Huppert, F. 2005. "Positive mental health in individuals and population." In F. Huppert, N. Baylis, & B. Keverne (Eds.). *The science of well-being (pp. 307 – 340)*. Oxford: Oxford University Press.

58. Jung, C.G. (translated by Hull, R.F.C.) 1990. The Archetypes and the Collective Unconscious. Princeton: Princeton University Press

59. Goleman, Daniel. 1997. *Emotional Intelligence*. New York: Bantam Dell.

60. Center for Disease Control and Prevention. May 3, 2017. *"Obesity and Overweight"*. National Center for Health Statistics.

61. LIFE Special Edition: Remembering Robin Williams 1951-2014. New York: Life Books

62. Cather Willa. O Pioneers! Vintage Books. 1992. New York: Random House Publishing.

63. Aristotle, Reeve C.D.C. 1998. *Politics.* Indianapolis: Hackett Publishing Company.

64. White, Emily. 2010. *Lonely.* Toronto: McClelland & Stewart.

65. Haworth, John. Evans, Stephen. 1995. "Challenge, skill and positive subjective states in the daily life of a sample of YTS students." *Journal of Occupational and Organizational Psychology, 68, 109-121.* UK.

66. Gray Peter, PhD. 2009. "Why Don't Students Like School?" Well, Duhhhh... *Phycology Today.* Posted Sept. 02, 2009.

67. Helliwell, John F., Layard, Richard and Sachs, Jeffrey D. 2018. *World Happiness Report.* New York: Sustainable Development Solutions Network.

68. Martela, F. et al. March, 2020. The Nordic Exceptionalism: What Explains Why the Nordic Countries Are Constantly Among the Happiest in the World. World Happiness Report 2020

69. Kalish, C. B. Bureau of Justice Statistics, US Department of Justice. May, 1988. *International Crime Rates.*

70. BlanchFlower David G. and Oswald Andrew. 2017. "DO HUMANS SUFFER A PSYCHOLOGICAL LOW IN MIDLIFE? TWO APPROACHES (WITH AND WITHOUT CONTROLS) IN SEVEN DATA SETS" NBER Working Paper Series, Working Paper 23724. *National Bureau of Economic Research.* August, 2017.

71. Thorne Deborah, Foohey Pamela, Lawless Robert M. & Porter Katherine.2018. "Graying of US Bankruptcy: Fallout from Life in a Risk Society." *Research paper, Indiana Legal Studies Research Paper No. 406,* data from Consumer Bankruptcy Project, posted 2018.

72. Easterlin, Richard. 1974. "Does Economic Growth Improve the Human Lot? Some Empirical Evidence." In Paul A. David and Melvin W. Reder, eds., *Nations and Households in Economic Growth: Essays in Honor of Moses Abramovitz,* New York: Academic Press, Inc.

73.   Hess, Abigail. 2017. "Here is Why Lottery Winners Go Broke." *CNBC Make it*, posted 25 Aug 2017.

74.   Lindqvist, Erik; Ostling, Robert; Cesarini, David. 2018. "Long-run Effects of Lottery Wealth on Psychological Well-being." *NBER Working Paper No. 24667*. Issued in May 2018.

75.   Singer, Peter. 1993. *HOW ARE WE TO LIVE? Ethics in an Age of Self-Interest*. Melbourne: Text Publishing .

76.   Bowskill, Derek and Linacre, Anthea. 1976. *THE MALE MENOPAUSE*. Brook House Press, UK.

77.   O'Connor, Peter. 1981. *UNDERSTANDING THE MID-LIFE CRISIS*. Melbourne (Australia): Sun Books.

78.   Mennatt, Richard; Tuskor, Morris and Anten, Jonathan. 1997. "Midlife Crises of Men at Age 50" quoted in *Critical Thinking About Research: Psychology and Related Fields* by Meltzoff, Julian, Nov.,1997.

79.   Conway, Jim. 1997. *MEN IN MIDLIFE CRISIS*. Colorado Spring (US): David C Cook.

80.   Ellenberger, H. 1970. *THE DISCOVERY OF THE UNCONSCIOUS*. New York: Basic Books.

81.   Frankl, V. 1959. *MAN'S SEARCH FOR MEANING*. Boston: Beacon Press

82.   Squires, Sally. 1999. "Midlife Without a Crisis" *Washington Post*, Monday, April 19, 1999; Page Z20 quoted results from research project by the John D. and Catherine T. MacArthur Foundation Research Network on Successful Midlife Development (MIDMAC).

83.   Sliwinski, Martin J.; Almeida, David M.; Smyth, Joshua and Stawski, Robert S. 2009. "Intraindividual change and variability in daily stress processes: Findings from two measurement-burst diary studies." *Psychol Aging*. 2009 Dec; 24(4): 828–840.

84.   Jaques E. Oct., 1965. "Death and the mid-life crisis". *International Journal of Psychoanalysis*. 46 (4), 502-14.

85.   Kolodiejchuk Brian, M. C. 2007. *MOTHER TERESA : Come Be My Light*. New York: Doubleday.

86.   Trump J. Donald, Leerhsen Charles. 1990. *Trump: Surviving At The Top*. New York: Random House Inc.

87.   Faiola, Anthony. 2005. "Sick of Their Husbands in Graying Japan." *Washington Post Foreign Service*. Monday, October 17, 2005

88.   World Bank. May 2014 GNI per capita, Atlas method (current US$).

89.   Simran, Bhargava; Madhu, Jain. 1989. "Mid-life crisis: Now, Indian men in their 40s confront traumatic life changes." *Indian Today*. Updated: October 22, 2013.

90.   Helliwell, John F., Layard, Richard and Sachs, Jeffrey D. 2012. *World Happiness Report*. New York: Sustainable Development Solutions Network.

91.   Ura, Dasho Karma: Alkire, Sabina. & Zangmo, Tshoki. 2011. *The 2010 Gross National Happiness Index*. The Centre for Bhutan Study. Thimphu. Bhutan.

92.   Cantril, H. 1965. *The Pattern of human concerns*. New Brunswick, New Jersey: Rutgers University Press.

93.   Sacks, Daniel W.; Stevenson, Betsey. & Wolfers, Justin. 2010. "Subjective Well-Being, Income, Economic Development and Growth", *the NATIONAL BUREAU OF ECONOMIC RESEARCH* Working Paper No. 16441, October, 2010.

94.   Oishi, Shigehiro; Kesebir, Selin and Diener, Ed. 2011. "Income Inequality and Happiness" *Psychological Science* 22(9), 1095 – 1100.

95.   Sidgwick, Henry;   Rawls, John. 1981. *the METHODS OF ETHICS*. Indianapolis: Hackett Publishing Company-86.

96.   Post, Stephen & Neimark, Jill. 2007. *WHY GOOD THINGS HAPPEN TO GOOD PEOPLE – HOW TO LIVE A LONGER, HEALTHIER, HAPPIER LIFE BY THE SIMPLE ACT OF GIVING*. New York: Broadway Books.

97.   Brickman & Campbell. 1971. "Hedonic relativism and planning the good society." pp. 287–302 in M. H. Apley, ed. *Adaptation Level Theory: A Symposium*. New York: Academic Press.

98.   Brickman P, Coates D, Janoff-Bulman R. 1978. "Lottery winners and accident victims: is happiness relative?" *Journal of Personality and Social Psychology* 36(8):917-27 · September.

99. Headey, B. W. and Wearing, A. J. 1989. "Personality, life events and subjective well-being: Toward a dynamic equilibrium model." *Journal of Personality and Social Psychology, 57,* 731-739.

100. Headey, B. W., Muffels, R. J.A., & Wagner, G., G. 2010. "Long-running German panel survey shows that personal and economic choices, not just genes, matter for happiness." *Proceedings of the National academy of Sciences of the United States of America, 107*(42), 17922-17926 (Oct. 19).

101. Clark, A. E., Diener, E., Georgellis, Y., & Lucas, R. E. 2008. "Lags and Leads in Life satisfaction: A test of the baseline hypothesis." *Economic Journal,* 118, 222-243.

102. Mehnert, T., Kraus, H. H., Nadler, R., & Boyd, M. 1990. "Correlates of life satisfaction in those with a disabling condition." *Rehabilitation Psychology, 35,* 3-17.

103. Lucas, R. E. 2007. "Long-term disability is associated with lasting changes in subjective well-being: Evidence from two nationally representative longitudinal studies." *Journal of Personality and Social Psychology, 92,* 717-730.

104. Headey, B.; Muffels, R.; Wagner, G. G. 2013. "Choices Which Change Life Satisfaction: Similar Results for Australia, Britain and Germany." *Soc Indic Res* 112:725 – 748.

105. Watson, David. 2,000. *Mood and Temperament.* New York: Guilford Press.

106. Wortman, C. B., & Silver, R. C. 1987. "Coping with irrevocable loss." In G. R. Vanderbos & B. K. Bryant (Eds.), *Cataclysms, crises, catastrophes: Psychology in action.* Washington, DC:APA

107. Isaacson, Walter. 2011. *Steve Jobs.* New York: Simon & Schuster.

108. Sutherland, Mark. 23 May 2015. "Taylor Swift interview: 'A relationship? No one's going to sign up for this'" *The Telegraph.* UK.

109. Barnett, Adrian. 2011. "Is 27 really a dangerous age for famous musicians? A retrospective cohort study." *The BMJ* (British Medical Journal). December 2011. UK.

110. *The Yellow Emperor's Classic of Medicine.* (trans. Ni, Maoshing. 1995. Boston: Shambhala.)

111. Benson, Herbert. 2002. "Meditation changes temperatures: Mind controls body in extreme experiments." *HARVARD GAZETTE ARCHIVES*.

112. Chalmers, Robert. 2011. "Happiest man on earth." *INDEPENDENT*. 21 September 2011, UK.

113. Chalmers, Robert. 2007. "Matthieu Ricard: Meet Mr. Happy." *INDEPENDENT*, 18 February 2007, UK.

ABOUT THE AUTHOR

James Z. Shaw is a researcher with Master of Science degrees in Chemical Engineering from universities in both China and the US. A small business entrepreneur, he is also a dedicated practitioner of Qigong, a traditional Chinese form of meditation in which he has accumulated over 20,000 hours of practice. His main philosophical interests are in the fundamental human understanding of reality.